Law For Home Improvers

and self-builders

All you need to know about buying, building and improving your home.

Guy Elyahou

NEW
HOLLAND

DEDICATION
For friends and family, past, present and future.

First published in 2004 by New Holland Publishers (UK) Ltd
Garfield House, 86–88 Edgware Road
London W2 2EA
London • Cape Town • Sydney • Auckland
www.newhollandpublishers.com

1 3 5 7 9 10 8 6 4 2

ISBN 1 84330 706 5

Senior Editor: Clare Hubbard
Editor: Ian Kearey
Designer: Casebourne Rose Design Associates
Illustrator: Sue Rose

Printed and bound by Kyodo Printing Co (Singapore) Pte Ltd.

ACKNOWLEDGEMENTS
Thanks to the eagle eyes of Daniel Ellison, Clarissa Feldman, Jenny Jackson and Robert Rome.

DISCLAIMER
This book is a general overview of the subject matters covered, and is for general guidance only. The author and the publishers do not assume legal responsibility for the accuracy of any statement contained in it. You must always seek independent professional advice on any legal matters. The author and the publishers take no liability for any statement contained in this book, nor any actions based upon any statement in this book. The views expressed in this book belong entirely to the author and not his employers.

The publishers have made every effort to ensure that the information contained in this book is correct at the time of going to press. The publishers cannot accept any liability for errors or omissions or changes in the details given.

Contents

4	**Introduction**	
6	*Chapter 1*	The Basics of English Law

10	PART ONE	**Buying, Planning and Developing Land**
11	*Chapter 2*	Buying Land
26	*Chapter 3*	Planning Considerations
53	*Chapter 4*	Environmental Law for Home Improvers and Builders
58	*Chapter 5*	Planning the Construction Works
68	*Chapter 6*	Professional Appointments and Construction Contracts
77	*Chapter 7*	Contract Law
89	*Chapter 8*	Clauses Specific to Building Contracts
98	*Chapter 9*	Contract and Site Administration
107	*Chapter 10*	Consumer Rights
113	*Chapter 11*	Negligence
117	*Chapter 12*	Nuisance
120	*Chapter 13*	Resolving Disputes
131	*Chapter 14*	Sale of Property
134	*Chapter 15*	Landlord and Tenant Relationships
140	*Chapter 16*	Misrepresentations

145	PART TWO	**Home Extensions and Renovations**
146	*Chapter 17*	Additional Planning Considerations for Home Improvements
156	*Chapter 18*	Party Walls
162	*Chapter 19*	The JCT Building Contract for Home Builders

165	*Appendix I*	Scottish Law
166	*Appendix II*	Latin Terms
167	Glossary	
170	Useful Contacts	
172	Index	

Introduction

Law is an unavoidable aspect of modern life. Whether you are buying or selling land, applying for planning consent, engaging builders or having a dispute with another party, you are going to be affected by some aspect of the legal system.

Most people have a natural and understandable fear of the legal system. This book breaks through the mystique of law by introducing you to some basic legal concepts that you are likely to encounter during your house-building or improvement project. The book is primarily based on English and Welsh law – there are a lot of similarities between English and Scottish law, but they are two different jurisdictions, and some of the differences between the two are examined in Appendix I (see page 165).

This book highlights the legal issues that you should consider when embarking on a building project. In more complex areas of law, such as the buying and selling of land, it provides an overview of the law to enable you to keep checks on, and have some control over, the progress of your transaction. Examples of some of the topics covered are the buying and selling of land, planning law, contract law, construction law and dispute resolution.

This book will give you:

- The confidence to comprehend a wide range of complex legal issues relevant to home building and improving.

- The ability to understand contracts on a variety of subject matters.

- The capability to successfully return faulty purchases.

- The competence to conduct basic legal disputes.

I have used the masculine gender to prevent unwieldy sentences. I have also used the terms "solicitor" and "lawyer" interchangeably.

The book is split into two parts. Part One covers the general areas of law that would be applicable to all self-build projects, whether building a new home from scratch or carrying out renovations. Part Two considers the specific issues that arise when carrying out works on an existing home. The vast nature of law means that I have only given an overview of the subject matter covered. Each chapter is written on a separate subject matter – you can either dip in and out of the book or read it from beginning to end so that when you embark upon your project you are armed with the requisite knowledge to successfully overcome whatever legal challenges are thrown your way.

CHAPTER 1

The Basics of English Law

This chapter is an introduction to the basics of English law. In order to understand some of the topics covered in this book you will need to have a basic grasp of the differences between civil law and criminal law, and how we have actually arrived at the laws that govern how we act in our society.

English law is unique in that it is steeped in its own history. This is unlike our Scottish and European neighbours whose laws are based on old Roman law. English law has also been widely exported. It forms the basis of the legal systems of many countries in the globe – not only those of the Commonwealth.

Unlike our American cousins, we do not have a single document that makes up our constitution. Our constitution is a pot-pourri of case law (sometimes dating back to the Middle Ages), government legislation and, more recently, European law.

For the purposes of this book, we shall consider that English law is split into criminal law and civil law.

Criminal law is generally the realm of the police and the Crown Prosecution Service (CPS). It is the CPS that takes the decision whether to prosecute a suspect based upon the evidence provided by the police. This may be of interest to us in a dispute with a neighbour where there may be criminal damage to property. Criminal law covers areas such as theft and physical violence. The burden of proof is for the Crown to prove that the suspect is guilty beyond all reasonable doubt. Magistrates and

Crown Courts are the key domains for the prosecution of criminal law. The only time we will look at criminal law in this book is when we look at planning law.

Civil law is what this book is all about. It is the law that governs human relationships, business transactions and civil disputes. Civil law is made up of:

● Thousands of previous cases on that particular subject matter.

● Legislation that is drafted by and voted upon by both the House of Commons and the House of Lords.

● European law.

In a civil dispute the burden is on the party bringing the action to prove his case on the balance of probabilities. The court system in civil disputes begins with the County Court, and goes through to the High Court, Court of Appeal, House of Lords and finally the European Court, which is the highest court in the United Kingdom.

Instructing solicitors

Solicitors are professionals who have trained long and hard to attain their status. They are also human – and some, while academically brilliant, may lack the social skills required to be effective problem solvers. This section gives you some guidance to ensure that you will instruct the best solicitor for your matter, at a competitive price.

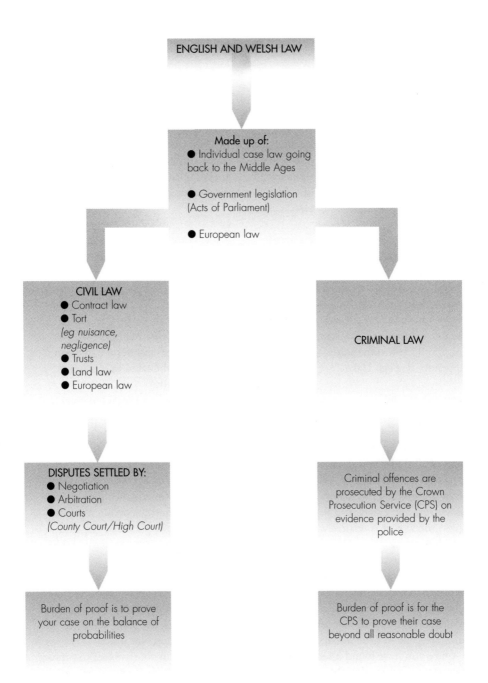

ENGLISH AND WELSH LAW

Made up of:
● Individual case law going back to the Middle Ages

● Government legislation (Acts of Parliament)

● European law

CIVIL LAW
● Contract law
● Tort
(eg nuisance, negligence)
● Trusts
● Land law
● European law

CRIMINAL LAW

DISPUTES SETTLED BY:
● Negotiation
● Arbitration
● Courts
(County Court/High Court)

Criminal offences are prosecuted by the Crown Prosecution Service (CPS) on evidence provided by the police

Burden of proof is to prove your case on the balance of probabilities

Burden of proof is for the CPS to prove their case beyond all reasonable doubt

English and Welsh law.

KEY POINTS

- Law in England and Wales is split into civil law and criminal law.

- Law is made up of:
  - individual case law decided by judges over hundreds of years;
  - legislation drafted by governments;
  - European law.

The legal industry has come a long way from Latin jargon, pinstriped suits and bowler hats. Lawyers who perpetuate the use of Latin are regarded with disdain, and are fortunately a dying breed. I have set out a short glossary of the most common Latin terms to assist you should you come across them (see Appendix II, page 166).

Shopping around

The first rule before instructing a solicitor is to shop around. Lawyers tend to fall into two camps – those who are jacks of all trades and those who are specialists in their area of law. The nature of your transaction or dispute will govern which you use. I suggest using the expert unless the matter is relatively straightforward.

To find a lawyer you should ask family and friends for recommendations. Failing that, contact the Law Society of England and Wales. Your local Citizens Advice Bureau may also be able to help you. (See page 171 for contact details.)

Once you have found a selection of lawyers you feel comfortable with, the next step is to meet them (if the matter is relatively straightforward a phone call should suffice); in particular, you should meet the person who is to undertake your work.

It is usual practice for a partner to "front" the transaction, whilst a competent assistant does the legwork (usually under the partner's supervision). Once you have found several firms you are comfortable with, you should obtain some quotes.

Fees

A few years ago getting competitive quotes from law firms was unheard of; however, the legal industry is increasingly competitive, and law firms are businesses like any other. When you receive the quote, check to see how it is calculated. For example, will you be charged on an hourly basis, and if so what are the rates, or is a lump sum proposed?

Sometimes your legal fees may be covered by an insurance policy, or you may be entitled to legal aid. If it is a dispute a law firm may make an offer of "No win, no fee". Finally, check to see what extras you may get charged for – VAT is additional with all lawyers but costs for disbursements such as faxes, telephone calls, photocopying and courier fees are not necessarily built into the original fee quote.

If you are undertaking a commercial transaction such as the sale and purchase of property I advise that you agree a separate fee in the event that the transaction does not proceed (known in the trade as an abortive fee) to prevent any potential arguments as to costs.

It is also advisable that you agree an

8

abortive fee with all your professionals. For example, you may have instructed surveyors, architects etc., all of whom will have incurred costs. If you have a good working relationship with your professional team they may be prepared to reduce their fees if there is the possibility of future work.

If you are going to court, your lawyer should advise you on the increased costs that may be incurred through instructing experts and employing barristers. In the event of you losing your case there is the risk that you will have to pay a proportion of the winning party's legal costs.

Teamwork

You and your lawyer will have to work as a team. A lawyer requires information and instructions on how to proceed. He cannot make decisions for you, only advise you on the risks associated with each option. A lawyer must always act independently and in the best interests of his client. You

---

KEY POINTS

● Ask around for several recommendations of individual lawyers and law firms; failing that, speak to the Law Society of England and Wales.

● Obtain quotes and meet lawyers to select the one you feel most comfortable with at a price that is right.

● Work as a team with your lawyer.

● If you are unhappy with your lawyer's work, contact the Law Society.

---

should contact the Law Society if you are not satisfied with your lawyer, or if your solicitor is acting negligently.

Buying, Planning and Developing Land

This part of the book encompasses the key legal topics for all self-builders and home improvers. Examples of the topics covered are the law relating to buying and selling property, contract law, planning applications, construction law, consumer rights, dispute resolution and the law relating to landlord and tenant relationships.

These chapters are not solely for those building a house from scratch. If you are proposing to build an extension or just carry out renovations you must consider the topics covered in Part One in addition to those covered in Part Two (which focuses solely on building extensions). The topics covered in Part One form the foundations upon which to understand the more advanced areas of law. For example, you will need to know basic law relating to buying and selling land before you can consider the implications of just buying part of a piece of land.

CHAPTER 2

Buying Land

After weeks and possibly months of agonising soul-searching, the decision has been made to hunt for that plot of land upon which to build your dream home. Plot buying (unlike house buying where estate agents are the norm) is unique in that self-builders tend to locate plots though more unconventional means.

Overview of the buying and selling process

The trade term that lawyers give to the process of buying and selling property is conveyancing. This chapter will give you an insight into what goes on in your lawyer's office, and also divulges how you can carry out some basic searches on the property before you instruct lawyers.

Conveyancing is traditionally carried out by solicitors; however, recent changes have opened up this work to professionals outside the legal industry. You can now instruct licensed conveyancers to act on your behalf, and you may even find that a solicitor will practise under the umbrella of a licensed conveyancer for reasons of professional indemnity insurance.

In England and Wales land is owned as either freehold land or leasehold land. However, in autumn 2003, new legislation was introduced permitting land to be held as "commonhold".

Leasehold and freehold land

Leasehold land, as its name suggests, is subject to the terms and conditions of a lease, which is usually between the leaseholder and the freeholder of the land.

A lease will have restrictions on what can and cannot be done to or in the property, and consent will have to be obtained from the freeholder for any works. A lease may also have restrictions on the sale and purchase of the leasehold property. This is in addition to any requirements from the mortgage provider, local authority and any existing restrictions on the land.

Leasehold land is where the freeholder grants a tenant a lease, typically for between 21 and 999 years (these are usually referred to as long leaseholds). Flats are typically leasehold property. A group of tenants can own a share of the freehold in the property. This usually means that a company has been set up by the tenants to own (and manage) the freehold, and each tenant owns a share in this company, some tenants may even be directors of it. Despite owning a share of the freehold, the tenants are still subject to a lease which governs what they can and cannot do to or in the premises.

Freehold land entitles the owner to own the land for eternity. Plots of land and houses are commonly freehold.

Once you have instructed your solicitor or licensed conveyancer, the process of buying and selling property is split into the following distinct stages:

Stage 1
Pre-exchange of contracts
Here, your solicitor investigates the legal characteristics of the property you are purchasing. It is also where you are at the greatest risk from incurring wasteful

11

costs if the deal becomes abortive. A seller and a buyer can pull out of the deal at any moment until the contracts are signed.

Stage 2
Exchange of contracts
This is the stage where both parties sign the contracts. Once signed, the seller is obligated to sell and the buyer is obligated to buy the premises. (There are exceptions to this; for example, where contracts are drafted so that any purchase is conditional upon certain events.)

Upon exchange the buyer will typically give the seller a deposit of between five–ten per cent of the purchase price.

Stage 3
Pre-completion
Once the contracts have been exchanged, there are typically 14–28 days for the purchase to complete. This time frame is open to negotiation. The solicitor will carry out some final searches to ensure that nothing untoward has cropped up in the interim period, and will also check that all monies are in place.

Simultaneous exchange and completion is possible.

Stage 4
Completion
This is the final stage of the transaction. The balance of the monies are paid to the seller, and the keys are handed over to the buyer.

Stage 5
Post-completion
The work post-completion rests with the solicitor. He will ensure that the relevant documents are stamped at the stamping office (Stamp Duty) and that the deeds are lodged with the Land Registry so that the new ownership of the land is a matter of public record.

Commonhold land
A new form of land ownership for England and Wales was introduced in autumn 2003. This is referred to as commonhold, and was implemented so that land ownership is more in line with Europe.

The commonhold provisions were introduced in the Commonhold and Leasehold Reform bill, which has changed hundreds of years of property law. The new act ensures that land can be held either as commonhold, leasehold or freehold. Commonhold will really benefit those people who live in flats or multi-occupied tenancies, for example, property owners who would otherwise be subject to restrictive leases for a term of years. The law's goal is to give such owners a greater freedom of ownership. In its most drastic form it gives the owner of a flat an effective freehold in that flat. The common parts (stairways, corridors etc.) will be owned and managed by a commonhold association which is likely to be a limited company, and each flat owner is likely to own a share in this association.

To summarise, the commonhold provisions simplify the ownership of property that would otherwise have been subject to leaseholds. It gives the owners security in land that is similar to a freehold interest.

Financing the purchase
As most home builders and improvers

know, a large part of any project is raising the finances for the venture. With hours spent on the phone to a variety of lending institutions in an attempt to get the best deal, you may be forgiven for thinking that each lender has its own diverse criteria. This is true up to a point. Ultimately, they all take their guidance from the Council of Mortgage Lenders (CML), the trade association for all mortgage lenders in the UK. The CML's members include banks, building societies and other residential mortgage lenders.

When deciding against what criteria to lend, most mortgage lenders will, in the first instance, take guidance from the CML. These guidance notes are on the Internet (www.cml.org.uk) and are regarded by many lawyers as the lending bible. Each individual mortgage lender will then bolt on their own criteria. Only when both these criteria are met will the funds be released. As a very rough guide, lenders will typically lend up to about 75 per cent of the purchase price and 95 per cent of the construction costs for a new-build project – up to a total of 75 per cent of the final valuation of the development. For a self-builder the funds

are usually released on an interim basis against progress of the works.

Mortgage lenders require some form of warranty from a recognised provider (such as the National House Building Council (NHBC), Premier Warranty or Zurich). They want this warranty to protect their investment should they need to repossess the property. It is in your interests to have one in place if you are thinking of reselling your property within ten years of its completion.

Most homebuyers approach a financial advisor, mortgage broker or existing high street lender to raise the bulk of the purchase (and construction) monies. When approaching financial advisors, ensure that they are independent. Many building societies and banks will refer you to what is known as a "tied financial advisor", who will only advise you on the products of that building society/bank.

Extra costs

It is not just the purchase price that you need to account for. Additional costs that must considered are professional fees (lawyers, estate agents and surveyors),

KEY POINTS

- Get quotes from licensed conveyancers as well as lawyers.

- Check to make sure that the professional indemnity insurance cover (of the lawyer/licensed conveyancer) is sufficient to cover any potential liability.

- Ensure that all your finances are in place so as not to delay the transaction.

- Having an offer accepted means nothing until contracts are exchanged.

search fees, Land Registry fees and Stamp Duty. If you are selling a second home, you will need to factor in any Capital Gains Tax that you may be liable for. This does not generally apply if you are selling your sole and principal residence. You should also ensure that you have between five–ten per cent of the deposit price ready to hand over on exchange.

Mortgages

There are two main types of mortgages:

- Interest repayment: here, you are paying off the interest of the loan; the capital sum will need to be paid in full at the end of the term. In order to pay off the capital sum you will pay monies into a investment vehicle such as an ISA or Endowment. The goal is that at the end of the term this investment will have matured and (in theory) be sufficient to pay off the capital sum. This is ideal if you are looking to hold on to the property for investment purposes or a short term.

- Capital repayments: this is where you pay off the entire capital sum (bit by bit) over the term of the loan.

Bridging loans can be used where you need to fill a short gap between selling your property and raising the finance to purchase the new property. If you do take out a bridging loan you may be eligible for tax relief.

It is common practice for your lawyer to act for the mortgage lender. One search that the solicitor must carry out on behalf of the mortgage lender is a bankruptcy search against the borrower.

The lender is unlikely to lend money to anyone who is subject to bankruptcy proceedings. The fees for acting on behalf of the lender are normally factored into your loan.

Pre-exchange of contracts

This is the most critical stage in the transaction and where most of the investigating takes place. This section will shed some light on the searches that get carried out on the property, the causes of most delays and how the terms of the draft contract are arrived at.

The pre-exchange phase is where your legal advisor will investigate the legal characteristics of the property that you are proposing to buy. Your lawyer will investigate things such as whether there are any rights of way affecting the land, any restrictions on the land, environmental concerns and the validity of any existing planning consents. These investigations are carried out before the contracts are signed.

Caveat emptor is a Latin phrase you may have come across – it means "buyer beware" and is of critical importance when investigating the property prior to an exchange of contracts. Once the contracts for the sale and purchase have been signed (exchanged) a binding contract is created between the contracting parties, and the buyer is bound to purchase the property with all its encumbrances.

What your lawyer will need from you

In the introduction I talked about how you and your lawyer need to work together. This is critical in the pre-exchange phase of the transaction. Your lawyer will need to know if you intend to build on the plot, if you plan to knock down the existing structure/house and build a new one, or even if you just wish to carry out home extensions and renovations. Your lawyer needs to know this so that he can modify his searches and queries, and ultimately draft the contract to reflect the realities of your purchase.

Advising couples

Your lawyer may only take instructions from his client. This means that if only one party is buying the property, then strictly speaking your lawyer can only take instructions from this party. If you are a couple, the lawyer will need instructions from the both of you. As a couple (or even a group of people), your lawyer will need to know whether you intend to purchase the land as joint tenants (couples only) or tenants in common (couples and groups of people). A tenancy in common can be converted into a joint tenancy and vice versa.

- Joint tenants: this is generally the manner in which married couples purchase a house so that if one partner dies the house automatically vests in the other party, even if there is no will. Each partner owns an equal and joint share in the property.

- Tenants in common: here, a group of people can own the property in different shares and can pass their share on to any party they wish.

Investigating the property

One of the first investigative steps is to ascertain whether the land is registered or unregistered. Most land in England and Wales is registered at the Land Registry – however, it is not uncommon, particularly when purchasing plots of land, to find that the land is unregistered. This means that the solicitor will have to investigate the root of the ownership of the land. This investigative process requires your solicitor to investigate numerous property deeds some of which may be

Case study

Alex is a partner in an engineering firm, married to Louise, a teacher. It would be prudent for the house to be purchased in Louise's name, as this will provide Alex and Louise with greater security in the unlikely event of Alex's partnership being the subject of litigation or Alex himself being the subject of bankruptcy proceedings. Conversely, the risk is that Alex would find himself in an uphill battle for the ownership of the house in the event of a divorce. It would be prudent for Alex to put a caution on the legal title of the property, restricting Louise's ability to sell the house.

several hundred years old. It can be a lengthy process. If the land is unregistered it will be registered (for its first registration) at the Land Registry upon completion.

Introduction to searches

The purpose of searches carried out on the property is to ascertain what risks are associated with the property that is being sold. Before you instruct solicitors you can carry out some informal searches yourself. For example, if the property is in a rural area locals are usually only too happy to talk about the owner of the site and its previous planning history (for example, rejected applications), environmental issues, flooding etc., that may be associated with the site. For example, if the property backs onto a brook it may be the case that careless DIY plumbing by your potential neighbours has resulted in foul water going down the rainwater pipes rather than into the sewage – something only a site visit would uncover.

The searches carried out by your lawyer investigate, amongst other things, whether there are any easements, restrictive covenants or planning restrictions attached to the land.

Easements

An easement is a right attached to the land. Easements usually allow the owner to exercise certain rights on the land – for example rights of way, rights to light and a right to water. Easements can also work against the property owner; for example, there may be a public footpath across a plot of land.

Restrictive covenants

A restrictive covenant is a burden that runs with the land (not the owner). It typically imposes some form of restriction upon the land; for example, not to build a dwelling on the land, not to alter the property without the consent of a third party and a prohibition on keeping pets. It can get problematic if the previous owner breached the restrictive covenants and the subsequent buyer is to take on this liability.

Planning history

Many plot buyers buy land subject to obtaining planning consent, or land that already has planning consent. Typically, land that already has planning consent may have what is known as outline planning consent. Again, the validity of the consent must be examined carefully. There is a finite amount of time within which the land must begin to be built upon. Your lawyer will also try to ascertain the planning history of the site to assist you with any future applications.

In addition to going to the site to inspect the property, you can log on to the Land Registry website (see page 170) and find out who owns the plot/house, when they purchased the plot, how much they paid for the property and the name of any mortgage lender. At the time of writing, it only costs £2 to carry out this most basic of searches. In order to read the information you will need Adobe Acrobat, which can be downloaded for free (www.adobe.com).

Local authority search

The local authority search is critical in the pre-exchange phase. The information that this search will uncover will be crucial when making the decision whether or not to purchase the land. The type of things that a local authority search can uncover runs into several pages; however, it will typically uncover the following information:

● Ownership of roads and sewers affecting the property.

● Planning applications (and any refusals of planning applications) – very useful for self-builders.

● Whether any compulsory purchase orders (CPOs) are in force or proposed.

● Any tree preservation orders (TPOs) that may be in place.

● If there are any road-widening schemes proposed.

If the purchaser is buying an existing property, the seller will complete what is known as a SPIF (Sellers Property Information Form). This gives additional details as to the nature of the property that are known to the seller.

Water authority search

This search ascertains who owns the sewers and whether there are connections to a main sewer. Because of the manner in which the water industry is set up, most searches have to go to the appropriate privatised water company, rather than the local authority.

Company search

Where the seller is a company, a company search is made to ensure, among other things, that the company exists and that it has the power to sell the land.

Bankruptcy search

If a bank is lending money on the purchase, the purchaser's solicitor will typically act for the lender in addition to the purchaser. This duality will require the solicitor to make a bankruptcy search against the buyer, as the lender is unlikely to lend money if bankruptcy proceedings are pending.

Additional searches

Plot purchases (as well as other residential purchases) may require the solicitor to make some more obscure searches:

● Coal mining search: this search is made if the property is in an area where coal mining has been (or is) being carried out. Problems relating to subsidence come out of such searches.

● Commons registration search: if the land is adjacent to a village green or common area (such as a park), this could cause problems with respect to obtaining planning consent.

● Whether any recent building works have been carried out on the land – if so one would expect to find a building contract, letters of appointment for the professionals and NHBC, Zurich (or similar) insurance cover.

● Environmental searches are increasingly common in plot purchases.

● Any matters of archaeological interest.

Survey

A building surveyor typically carries out the survey to ascertain the structural integrity of the property. The survey highlights any risks that may not be apparent to the layman. Mortgage lenders also insist upon a survey on the physical state of the property, as they want to know the value of their security to assess the size of the loan. It is absolutely critical that if there are any specific concerns that you have in relation to the property you express these in writing to your surveyor – for example, whether the property is located under any known flight paths. Different runways (and holding patterns) change in use over the year, so it may not always be apparent whether the property is affected.

Conditional contracts

It is not uncommon for a solicitor to prepare a conditional contract for house builders buying a plot of land. This means that the sale and purchase of the plot or house will be conditional upon a certain event occurring.

Examples of conditional events are:

● Obtaining planning consent for the purchaser.

● The seller needing to obtain vacant possession of the premises.

● Environmental clean-ups.

● Where the buyer has not completed his searches, or his client's finances are not in place.

In practical terms this means that the contracts will be exchanged, but there is no obligation upon the buyer to complete the purchase until the conditional event has occurred. This could be some months down the line. The responsibility for getting planning consent usually rests with the purchaser; however, it is possible for the seller to take on this burden. It may even be in the seller's interest to take on this responsibility because he will have a greater control over the completion of the purchase.

Where plots are sold conditional upon planning consent, the parties have to agree upon:

● Whether is it outline or detailed planning consent that is being applied for.

● Who is to pay for the planning application.

● What conditions are deemed acceptable in order for the buyer to commit to the transaction.

As ideal as conditional contracts sound for plot buyers, they are strongly resisted by sellers as they introduce an element of uncertainty into the transaction. Many legal advisors acting on behalf of a seller will tend to resist conditional contracts (unless there is some obvious advantage).

The uncertainty of a conditional contract is remedied by having a fixed date for completion (long stop date), after which if the specified event has not occurred, both parties can walk away from the deal. It is more common for the seller to sell the plot with outline planning consent. This additional certainty for the buyer is usually reflected in an increased sale price.

Chained transactions

These are every lawyer's nightmare: chained transactions are where you have several independent parties each involved in the sale and purchase of a separate property. The trick is for each party to exchange at the same time so that no party is left with having sold their property but not having bought one.

For example: A is selling a house to B, and is also buying from C. B is buying a house from D, who is buying from E, and E is selling to F. Do you see the problem? Each party has to carry out their own searches, has their own legal advisors and mortgages to both redeem and take out, and of course monies to transfer – all on the same day! A, B, C, D and E are usually couples who are keen to get the transaction going, but F is usually a first-time buyer who is not at risk of having nowhere to live if there is some form of delay. The trick is not to exchange on any property without having one to buy. The Law Society has a system in place for lawyers to complete such chained transactions.

Exchange of contracts
Terms of the contract
The contract will follow the standard terms prepared by the Law Society. However, as no two purchases are ever the same your lawyer is likely to draft some additional terms and delete others, all of which reflect your transaction. These terms are negotiated and the usual bargaining factors come into play, depending upon which party has the upper hand. If you are buying a house from an existing national house builder, the terms of the contact are unlikely to be negotiable.

The terms and conditions of the mortgage will also be agreed. I strongly suggest that you read the small print: the terms and conditions of the mortgage may have restrictions on any renovation of the property, and will certainly have guidelines and standards to adhere to if you are carrying out any renovations – for example using only CORGI-registered plumbers, and having a NICEIC certificate for the electrical work.

Prior to the exchange of contracts the purchase price must be agreed and the buyer must have the agreed deposit ready to send to his solicitor. The solicitor will also ensure that the lender is satisfied that the transaction can go ahead. The deposit is usually five–ten per cent of the purchase price. There is no legal requirement (outside the terms of the contract) to pay a deposit, but it is common practice. If interest has accrued on the deposit then this should be taken off the balance when the monies are passed on to the seller.

Plot purchases usually attract a request from an estate agent for a preliminary deposit (to be paid to the estate agent) as a goodwill gesture. You should be wary of this. Whilst the vast majority of estate agents are honest brokers, they are not governed by the same regulations that lawyers are. It is not unknown for such "goodwill" deposits, together with the purported "estate agent", to disappear into the ether. (Estate agents are required, as a matter of law to insure client's money.) If a preliminary deposit is requested, it is advisable to check the estate agent's trading background and, more importantly, whether the deposit is refundable.

Preparing the contract

Your solicitor makes the final checks to ensure that all the searches have been completed and that the results are satisfactory. Your lawyer also checks that the mortgage is in place and that the terms of the contract have been agreed.

The most critical factors that you, as a purchaser, will need to consider and advise your lawyer upon are:

● The purchase price.

● The amount of the deposit, taking into account interest earned.

● Confirmation and availability of the mortgage and insurance.

● The date for completion (when the remaining sums are handed over to the seller).

● Any additional conditions (such as planning and conditional contracts) that are particular to you or your transaction. In plot purchases I suggest examining any plans yourself and possibly visiting the site with

them to ensure that what you are purchasing corresponds with your expectations.

● Manner of signing the contract. Normally the parties involved in the transaction will sign the contract. A solicitor can only sign on behalf of his client if he has express written authority to do this.

Insurance

Your solicitor will advise you whose responsibility it is to insure the premises once the contracts have been exchanged. Typically, it is the seller's responsibility to insure the property after exchange. This means that the buyer is relying upon the seller to maintain the insurance of the premises that the buyer has contracted to buy. If you are buying a plot of land, this is unlikely to concern you. However, if you are purchasing a house you may want greater control and you can request that the responsibility to maintain the insurance rests with you (the purchaser) once contracts have been exchanged.

Exchange of contracts

A solicitor must not exchange contracts unless he has his client's express permission to do so. If you are not available, you can give written instructions to your lawyer to execute the contract on your behalf. If you need to execute the mortgage deed, you need to prepare a (limited) power of attorney for your lawyer to execute the mortgage deed on your behalf.

In times gone by there used to be a physical exchange of contract. Very few solicitors do this now, and a more mundane "exchange" of contracts takes place over the telephone in accordance with the Law Society's guidelines. Postal exchange is also possible, but very uncommon.

Once the contract is exchanged (and assuming that there are no outstanding conditions), there is a binding agreement between the parties for the sale and purchase of the property. A failure to complete is a breach of contract, and the remedies available are considered at the end of this chapter.

Post-exchange

The time frame between exchange and completion is usually 14–28 days. It is possible for exchange and completion to occur on the same day – in order for this to happen everything (including the finances) will need to be in place. The seller or purchaser may want to change the length of the period between exchange and completion depending upon their personal circumstances and financial position.

The key activities that take place post-exchange are additional searches and getting the funding for the purchase in place. Your solicitor will also prepare the document which effects the transfer (purchase deed).

As most searches have been carried out before exchange your legal advisor should only need to carry out a selection of minor searches (some of them repeat searches) as close as possible to the completion date. This is to ensure that no changes as to the status of the property have occurred between exchange and completion.

The purchase deed is the document

that effects both the purchase and the ownership of the property. It is prepared by the legal advisors and signed by the purchaser. Your legal advisor will explain to you, in detail, the significance of the purchase deed and the provisions contained in it. Another person can sign on behalf of the purchaser providing a valid power of attorney is provided. If a company is purchasing the property the company seal may be affixed, but a director and either a second director or a secretary of the company must sign the document.

Your solicitor then prepares a completion statement setting out the finances for the final stages of the transaction. Typically, the completion statement will provide for:

● Purchase price less any deposit paid.

● Apportionment of costs such as council tax, services bills, etc.

● Money payable for items such as a fridge, washing machine etc., known in the trade as fittings.

● Stamp Duty.

● Land Registry fees.

● The mortgage and any fees associated with it.

● Professional fees.

If you are the seller, your lawyer will provide your mortgage lender with a redemption statement that sets out the exact amount of money required to redeem your mortgage. This will be deducted from the monies that the buyer pays for the purchase.

Completion

Before the date of completion the buyer's solicitors will have received the results of the final searches. It is prudent for the buyer's solicitors to have the balance of the purchase price in their client account before the date of the completion. This is to allow for any unforeseen hiccups sod's law has a nasty habit of appearing on completion days.

The completion itself is a very uneventful affair if everything is in place; all it really involves is the transferring of funds from the buyer's solicitors to the seller's solicitors. In practical terms, this must be done on the morning of the completion day, to ensure that the funds are not held up in the banking clearing system. Funds usually leave your lawyer's office before 3pm to ensure that completion can take place on the same day.

If completion does not take place, the contract provides for a daily rate (and interest) payable by the party in default. It may be the case that the buyer has not been able to arrange the finances or the seller has not been able to obtain vacant possession of the property.

Once the seller's solicitor has confirmed that the funds have been received, the buyer is entitled to the keys and, as far as he is concerned, that is the end of the matter.

Post-completion

The activities that take place post-completion are the responsibility of the legal advisors. The buyer's solicitor ensures that the proper documents are sent to the Land Registry, and the documents are stamped at the stamping office. The mortgage lender normally holds the deeds. Both solicitors then send out bills for their work in completing the transaction.

Delays

A common complaint made to legal advisors relates to delays in the process of buying and selling property. There are several reasons for this, and the blame does not necessarily rest with the lawyer. A solicitor's primary duty is to act in the best interests of his client, therefore if the other party has instructed his lawyer to delay the process, there is little your lawyer can do. Also, all professionals are at the mercy of local authorities and the Land Registry when it comes to providing information.

A common cause of delay is waiting for the paperwork and deeds for the property from other lawyers and the mortgage lender. The mortgage lender will not release these deeds without the seller's written authority – more paperwork. Once they have agreed to release these deeds, the lender will have to retrieve them from a safe storeroom, usually held by an external contractor. All these things take time.

For example, your solicitor cannot carry out any searches until he has a plan of the property. He cannot get the plan until he has the deeds. The mortgage lender usually holds the deeds. The lender needs authority to release them and then to locate and send them.

Search results also take time. Some local authorities and third parties can be

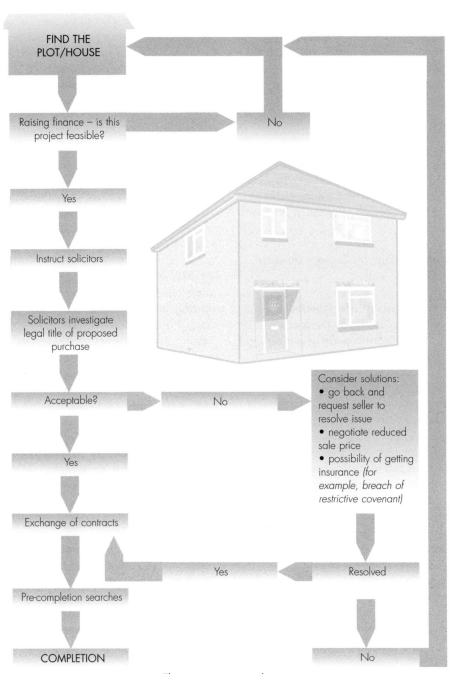

FIND THE PLOT/HOUSE

Raising finance – is this project feasible? → No

Yes

Instruct solicitors

Solicitors investigate legal title of proposed purchase

Acceptable? → No → Consider solutions:
• go back and request seller to resolve issue
• negotiate reduced sale price
• possibility of getting insurance (*for example, breach of restrictive covenant*)

Yes

Exchange of contracts

Yes ← Resolved

Pre-completion searches

COMPLETION   No

The process to completion.

very efficient and get their responses back within a matter of days, while others can take up to two months. If the transaction drags on for months, many searches may have to be carried out again, at an additional cost.

Remedies

The rights available to either the buyer or seller in a failed transaction only arise once the contracts have been exchanged. The remedies are based on those that are available for breach of contract. You can either:

● Make a claim for damages (financial compensation).

● Request an order for "specific performance", where the courts compel the other party to complete their part of the agreement.

The basics for a breach of contract are that the claim must generally be brought within six years of the contract being entered into.

The amount of damages that the aggrieved party is entitled to is the sum of money that puts them in the position that they would be in had the contract been properly performed, together with any reasonably foreseeable consequential losses that were contemplated by the parties at the time the contract was entered in to.

For example, if you are buying a plot and are going to order materials after exchange but before completion, you should inform the seller of this so that they are aware of your potential losses. Alternatively, if you are in a chain and the purchase of your new house is dependent upon the sale of your existing house, then the parties involved in the transaction should be aware of this risk. Contrary to popular belief, you cannot claim for mental distress.

Another remedy is known in the trade as "specific performance". This is where the courts compel a party to complete the transaction. It is not uncommon for this remedy to be applied in sale-and-purchase transactions.

The most common breach of contract is a delay in achieving the completion date. In the first instance, you will not normally be entitled to terminate the contract because of a delay to the completion date. However, the contract should allow for a daily rate of damages to be payable to the aggrieved party.

False representations that induce a party to enter into a contract may amount to a breach of contract. The key elements are that the statement was false, it induced the other party to enter into the contract and that the aggrieved party suffered a loss. These statements may be made innocently, fraudulently or negligently.

Usually only a party to a contract can sue, and this should be the party that has suffered the loss. However, a recent change in English law provides that in limited circumstances a third party can bring an action if the contract was to infer some benefit upon them.

SUMMARY

In this chapter we have examined the legal process in buying and selling property.

The key stages in any transaction are:

✎ Pre-exchange of contracts.

✎ Exchange of contracts.

✎ Pre-completion.

✎ Completion.

✎ Post-completion.

● Once contracts are exchanged, there is a binding contract in place compelling the parties to complete the sale and purchase.

● There are many third parties involved in the transaction. These can be the cause of delays.

● Civil law remedies for breach of contract are available to an aggrieved party where contracts have been exchanged but the sale and purchase fails to complete. These remedies may be financial, or may even compel the other party to sell (or buy) the property as agreed.

● A third party who is not a party to the original contract may bring an action if it is intended that the contract infers some benefit upon them.

CHAPTER 3

Planning Considerations

Planning consents

In an ideal world, you would have bought your dream house or plot of land and go straight to the builder's merchant to load up the van with your tools and materials ready to start the works. Unfortunately, it is not that simple. Your project may require planning consent from the local authority, and will also require building regulations approval – planning consent and building regulations approval being different consents.

There are varying levels of bureaucracy for each local authority, and some authorities are more accommodating and helpful than others when it comes to getting that critical planning consent.

On average there are about 550,000 planning applications in England and Wales. Almost 50 per cent are for householder developments, and about 90 per cent of these are usually approved. In practice 65 per cent of these applications are approved within eight weeks. In the vast majority of cases, the planning consent that is granted is tied to the land as opposed to the owner of the land. Accordingly, if you buy land with existing planning consent, this consent passes to you, the new owner, with the land. There are very few exceptions where the planning consent may be tied to the owner.

Throughout this chapter I refer to the local authority as the authority being responsible for granting any planning applications. You should be aware, however, that in a few cases (usually outside metropolitan areas) your local authority might not be the relevant authority for planning issues. In such cases, you may need to phone around to find out who is the appropriate planning authority for your area.

Does a development require planning consent?

With the exception of listed buildings and Conservation Areas, the law relating to planning is enshrined in the Town and Country Planning Act 1990, which is an extensive act with approximately 340 sections. The extracts in this section are from this act.

If you are building an extension to your home, your project may fall within an exemption not requiring you to apply for planning consent. A recently purchased plot of land may also have been sold with outline planning consent, thus giving you approval "in principle" and some guidance as to what the local authority considers acceptable for your development.

The first step is whether you are considered, in the eyes of the law, to be carrying out a "development" on the land. The general rule is that if you are going to be developing your land you need planning consent.

For the purposes of planning regulations, a "development" means *"the carrying out of building, engineering, mining or other operations in over or under land or making of any material change in the use of any buildings or other land"*.

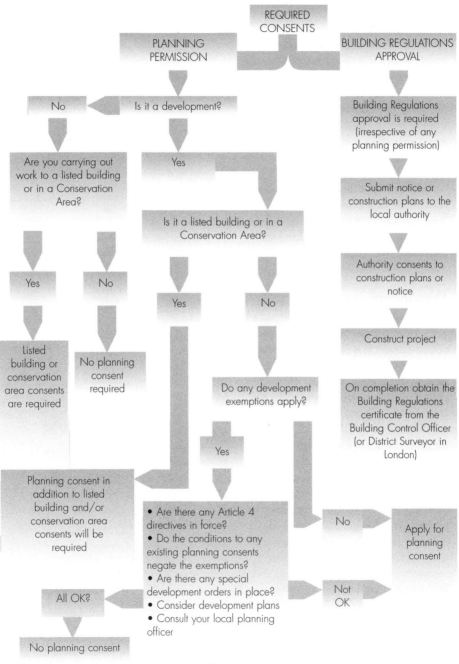

Consents.

The demolition of a dwelling house (and adjoining houses), rebuilding, structural alterations or additions to the building and *"Other operations normally undertaken by a builder"* are considered to be a development for the purposes of planning regulations.

However, if you are only carrying out works that affect the interior of the building or works which do not materially affect the building's external appearance, you will not generally require planning consent as these activities are not considered to be a development. (However, you may still need to obtain additional consent if the building is listed or in a Conservation Area.)

Listed building.

Demolition

Demolition is not generally regarded as being development. For homebuilders and improvers it is likely that the works you are intending to carry out will be outside this general rule and will require you to obtain planning consent for the demolition works. If you are demolishing any of the buildings shown on pages 28–29 you will need consent.

The Building Act 1984 imposes additional obligations upon the self-builder where demolition is concerned. Section 80 of the Act requires notice to be given to the local authority of any intended demolition of the whole or part of a building, except a demolition:

● Pursuant to a demolition order.

● Of an internal part of a building, where the building is occupied and it is intended that it should continue to be occupied.

Scheduled monument.

Building in a Conservation Area.

Dwelling house or building adjacent to dwelling house.

Buildings not exceeding 50 cu m in volume.

● Of a building that has a cubic content (as ascertained by external measurement) of not more that 1,750 cu ft, or where a greenhouse, conservatory, shed or prefabricated garage forms part of a larger building, of that greenhouse, conservatory, shed or prefabricated garage.

● An agricultural building.

Change of use

Planning consent is also required if you are materially changing the use of a building. What constitutes a "material" change in use depends upon your individual circumstances. For example, if the property was once an industrial warehouse and you now plan to convert it into a house, you will require planning permission allowing you to change the use of the building. This is a very simplistic overview of the change of use provisions. Much of the law on this topic is governed not by legislation drafted by parliament, but by individual cases over time.

Examples of use classifications are:

● A1: shops

● A2: professional advisors

● A3: food and drink

● B2: general industrial

● B8: storage and distribution

● C3: dwelling houses

29

Class A1 (shops).

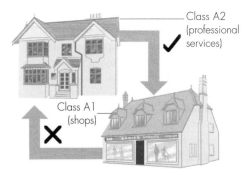

Class A2 (professional services).

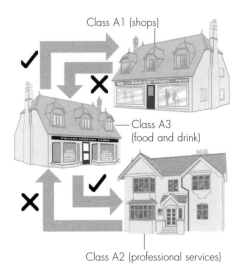

Class A3 (food and drink).

The classification of use that you are most likely to come across is Class C (residential uses) and in particular Class C3: dwelling houses. For these purposes, a dwelling house is defined as *"a house that is used as a dwelling (whether or not as a sole or main residence); by a single person or by people living together as a family or by not more than six residents living together."*

Neither changes within a class nor the use of any building within the grounds of your house, for purposes incidental to the enjoyment of the house, are considered a change of use (and are therefore not considered to be a development requiring planning consent).

Class C1 (hotels – no significant care).

Class C2 (residential schools).

Summary of the most common uses and the permitted changes of the use classes order:

CLASS	PERMITTED CHANGE *note: permitted changes are one way and cannot be made in reverse)*
A1 *(shops)*	No permitted change
A2 *(professional services)*	Permitted change to A1
A3 *(food and drink)*	Permitted change to A1 or A2
C1 *(hotels – where there is no significant care)*	No permitted change
C2 *(residential schools)*	No permitted change
C3 *(dwellings, meaning six or less residents living together as a family)*	No permitted change
D1 *(non-residential institutions such as churches)*	No permitted change

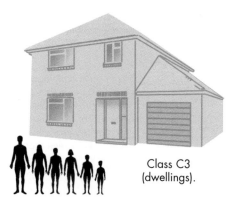

Class C3 (dwellings).

Class D1 (non-residential institutions).

Once you have established that you are carrying out a development on the land – either by way of the building works or because you are materially changing the use of the land – you may need planning consent. I say "may", because certain types of development are exempt from requiring planning consent. These exemptions are set out in the Town and Country Planning (General Permitted Development) Order 1995. This is available on the Internet (see page 171).

The Town and Country Planning (General Permitted Development) Order 1995

Schedule 2 of The Town and Country Planning (General Permitted Development Order) 1995 provides for certain exemptions for a development without you having to apply for planning permission. Schedule 2 of the Order is broken down into a number of sections.

For the house builder, the most important sections are Parts 1 and 2, which give consent for certain developments within the curtilage of a dwelling house and for minor operations. The illustrations on this page are examples of developments permitted by Part 1.

These are only a small selection of the permitted activities; it is imperative that you read the actual section of the act and get expert advice.

Limitations for Part 1 activities are usually placed upon the location of the building (for example, if it is in a

Enlargement, improvement or alteration to the house.

Additions or alterations to the roof only.

Provision of a building (including a swimming pool) for any purpose incidental to the enjoyment of the house, or the maintenance, improvement or alteration of such a building.

Erection of a porch.

Installation of a satellite antenna.

conservation area, an area of outstanding natural beauty, national parkland or if it is listed), the increase in cubic content of the house, increase in height, distance from the highway and the total area covered by all the buildings. If these development activities exceed the thresholds set out in the Order, then there are no applicable exemptions and planning consent will be required. These are covered in greater detail later on in this book.

Examples of developments permitted by Part 2 works are shown in the illustrations on this page.

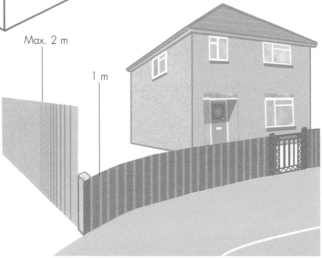

Construction of a means of access to a highway (which is not a trunk or classified road).

Painting the exterior of a building (provided it is not for any form of advertisement).

Erection, construction, maintenance, improvement or alteration of a gate, fence, wall or other means of enclosure (provided they are not more than 1 m high if they are adjoining the highway or 2 m in any other case).

Max. 2 m

1 m

Exemptions and checks

If your works fall into one of the above exemptions, there are some additional checks that you should tick off before being confident that you do not need any planning consent.

● Check that your proposed development falls within the limitations of the relevant permitted development category (you must refer to the Order).

● Check existing planning consents relating to the property as to whether there are any conditions attached to them. Sometimes these will restrict your ability to take advantage of the permitted development rights.

● Check with the local authority to ensure that no Article 4 is in force. Article 4 allows the local authority to remove any of the permitted development rights listed above.

● Check your deeds to make sure that there are no restrictions on you to develop the land (known as restrictive covenants).

● Check with the council to ensure that there are no special development orders in place. This may affect the exercise of permitted development rights.

● Try to carry out a physical inspection of the site.

● Obtain copies from your local authority of the development plans and any non-statutory plans that they may have produced.

● If the land is agricultural, you may need to fill in an agricultural holding certificate. The reason for this is that agricultural land is subject to special statutory controls.

● You may want to consider having an informal chat with the planning office at your local authority. However, there are obvious advantages and disadvantages in adopting this approach.

SUMMARY

If you are developing land or changing its use, you must consider whether you need to obtain planning permission. As discussed, you will not always need planning consent, and I have listed a small number of those exemptions in this section.

Making a planning application

It is likely that you will have to get involved with making an application for planning permission at some stage of the development. This is particularly true if you are building a house from scratch (rather than building an extension, in which case you may fall into one of the exemptions).

It is also likely that you will make your own planning application to your local authority, in which case you need as much ammunition as possible to ensure that your application is successful. If you have instructed an architect, it is usually within the scope of his services to make the application(s) on your behalf – make sure this is agreed before you employ him.

Remember that the purchase of the property can be made conditional upon you receiving suitable planning consent – in which case, if the application fails or has onerous conditions, you are not obliged to buy the property or plot.

Applying for planning permission

To avoid making a rod for your own back, consider whether or not you actually need to make a planning application. Assuming you do, the first step is to gather as much information as possible about the site; for example maps, historical data and the previous usage of the site. You will also need to obtain a copy of the development plan for the area from your local authority, as well as any other plans/guidance notes that they have that may affect your development. It also helps to pay a visit to the site and buy the locals a few beers – many of them are likely to have had firsthand experience of their local planning officers, and such insights will pay dividends.

This may be a good opportunity to informally discuss your proposal with the planning officer, who may also be able to provide you with some useful information. For example, it may be that an application has been made in the past and was rejected. The officer may then tell you the reasons why it was rejected, and you can modify your application accordingly.

The next step is to obtain the correct application form from the local authority. Each local authority has its own forms, which are free of charge. Before completing the form you will need to consider what type of permission you are going to request. There are two types: full and outline permission.

Outline permission requires a general description of the development and its features; you also need to submit a plan showing the various boundaries of the project. If successful, outline permission means that the local authority has approved your plan in principle. If your development is relatively small, for example if you are only applying for planning consent in order to build an extension, then you will need to be sure that the plans for your applications are detailed. It is possible that the local authority will not accept applications for outline planning consents for relatively small works and a full application will be required.

If you obtain outline permission, the local authority will list some "reserved matters", which must be approved by the authority before the development can proceed. Typically, they are concerned with the siting, design, external appearance, access and landscaping of your project.

Sending in the planning application

The application form, fee, General Permitted Development Order (GPDO) certificate, Agricultural Holdings certificate, plans, letters, drawings etc. are sent (usually in triplicate) to the appropriate local authority governing the development. You complete the GPDO and Agricultural Holdings certificates.

The GPDO form relates to the ownership of the land, while the Agricultural Holdings certificate requires you to make a statement as to whether or not the development is to take place upon agricultural land.

The local planning authority will then give notice of your intended planning application to the general public and will consult various organisations about your application. Depending upon the scope of your development, the notice will either be a site notice, an advert in the local paper or a notice served on adjoining owners – or perhaps all three.

Decision time

The local planning authority has the discretion to make three types of decisions on your application:

● A refusal.

● Permission that is subject to certain conditions.

● Unrestricted permission.

In addition, the planning authority may only be prepared to grant permission if the applicant enters into a legal agreement with the planning authority in which the applicant usually promises to carry out certain other works or accept certain restrictions on the future use of the land (this is known as a Section 106 agreement).

When reaching its decision, the authority must take into consideration its development plan and other material considerations. The development plan is something that you can obtain, but what are these "other material considerations"? The definition is arbitrary; it is not something that is set in stone. Material considerations are made up of cases dating back over 30 years. Examples are:

● Previous planning history of the site.

● Access and transport implications.

● Environmental considerations.

● Impact upon the neighbours.

You are likely to get the decision within eight weeks of your application.

Once you get consent, you need to be aware that planning permission belongs to the land, not the owner. Therefore, if you sell the plot, you sell it with the benefit of the planning consent and the burdens of the conditions that are attached to it. It is only in exceptional cases that planning consent is stated to be personal to the owner of the land.

Once you get full planning consent, you have to start the building works within five years, otherwise you will find that the consent has lapsed.

If the consent is for outline permission, there are two time limits to consider: you must apply for approval of the reserved matters within three years of the date that the outline permission has been granted; and you must begin the development within either five years of the date of the outline permission, or within two years of the approval of the reserved matters, whichever is the earlier.

In the eyes of the law, for the purposes of the time limits set out above, the (text continues on page 38)

Construction work in the course
of erecting a building.

Digging for foundations.

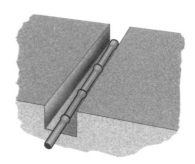

Laying a pipe or commencing
works on a road.

Demolition works.

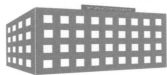

Material change
in use of the land.

Commencement of development can be signified by the above.

37

commencement of your development can be signified by:

● Any construction work in the course of erecting a building.

● Demolition works.

● Digging for the foundations.

● Laying a pipe, commencing works on a road.

● Material change in use of the land (in accordance with the consent).

Only one of these activities needs to occur in order to stop the clock in relation to the expiry of the planning consent granted. This is of particular relevance if you have recently purchased a plot that was granted planning consent some years prior to your purchase – you may need to commence the development without delay in order to stop the clock.

You can apply for renewal of a planning consent, but this must be done before the expiry of the existing consent, otherwise you will have to apply from scratch. Renewals are generally a straightforward affair, although it could get tricky if in the interim period there has been a drastic change in the local authority's development plan and your proposal no longer fits in with what they want for that locality.

Once you have commenced the works and the works are not completed within the time period set out by the local authority in the planning consent, they may issue you with a completion notice if they feel that you are not going to complete your project within a reasonable amount of time. A completion notice gives you a minimum of 12 months within which to complete the development.

SUMMARY

Not every development is going to require planning consent; it may be that an informal chat with the local planning officer will pay dividends. It would also be prudent to make any purchase of a plot subject to the attainment of planning consent for your project. This is likely to delay the purchase but will ensure that you are not left with a plot that cannot be granted planning consent because of some unforeseen reason.

Planning authorities have to act within set guidelines when considering your planning application. They cannot act unreasonably, and they must give their reasons when granting consent subject to conditions.

UK planning laws are set for a radical overhaul around 2005–2008. However, with the law as it currently stands there are certain developments that are permitted by the planning acts and do not require planning consent provided they are carried out within the parameters set out in the planning acts.

Section 106 agreements

No chapter on planning would be complete without a discussion on Section

106 agreements. In layman's terms a Section 106 agreement is a horse trade – an agreement that sets out the trade-off between the local authority and the developer for the local authority giving its consent to the development. It is called a Section 106 agreement because it relates to Section 106 of the Town and Country Planning Act 1990.

A Section 106 agreement is effectively a contract between the local authority and the developer. The agreement allows the local authority to impose conditions that would not necessarily be permitted by the planning acts – for example, a planning condition that is attached to a planning consent cannot require you to pay money to the local authority, relinquish land or carry out works to land that you do not own. In a Section 106 agreement these restrictions do not apply to the local authority. However, the local authority does not have carte blanche as to what conditions it can impose.

The conditions imposed by the local authority in a Section 106 agreement must be:

● Relevant to planning.

● Necessary to make a proposal acceptable in land use terms.

● Fair and reasonable in scale having regard to the development proposed.

● Reasonable in all other respects.

The scope of what can be incorporated in a Section 106 agreement is set out in Section 106 of the act – if it is proposed that you enter into a Section 106 agreement I strongly recommend that you read the act and get professional advice.

If the obligation is manifestly unreasonable, it would be considered beyond the powers of the local authority to impose it (even if the developer agreed to it). A local authority cannot force you into agreeing a Section 106 agreement – the whole ethos is that these are voluntary agreements. You can make an appeal to the Lands Tribunal if you are unhappy with the conditions imposed in the Section 106 agreement.

Appealing against an adverse planning decision

House building, home extensions and planning legislation are uneasy partners at the best of times, and it may be that you find yourself having to appeal against the planning decision that was refused, or appealing against the conditions that were attached to the planning consent.

You can employ a professional, such as a lawyer or planning specialist, to appeal the refusal or conditions. However, it does no harm for you to be aware of your rights and the stages that the professional will be taking when making the appeal on your behalf.

Time limits

Only the person who originally applied for the planning consent can appeal against the decision. This can be a key issue, particularly if the original application was made in the name of an agent who is no longer around, or the land has changed hands since the application was made. The appeal is made to the Secretary of State for the Environment on a special form issued by the Planning Inspectorate.

Examples of what the applicant can appeal against are:

● Failure of the planning authority to give a decision within the required time limits. An appeal can be brought on the basis of a deemed refusal if the planning authority has not made a decision within eight weeks, unless this time period is extended with the applicant's agreement.

● Any conditions to which the planning consent is subject to.

● Refusal of planning consent.

The form must be completed and sent to the Planning Inspectorate within the specified time limit. The form is split into six sections and is likely to require you to send in additional documentation with your appeal, such as plans, drawings and correspondence. You must appeal within three months of the notice of the planning decision or the date on which the authority is deemed to have refused the application.

The appeal

An appeal can be heard either in a hearing or an inquiry, where you or your legal representative make oral representations, or by written representations only.

When completing the form you are given the opportunity to indicate your preference as to what type of hearing you prefer. Written representations is an appeal based solely on documentation:

no oral evidence is permitted, but the planning inspector visits the site before making a decision.

The vast majority of appeals are dealt with in this way; recent reports put the figure at 80 per cent. The reason is because they tend to be much cheaper and quicker than having oral representations; additionally, the majority of appeals do not justify oral hearings. However, written representations are only permitted where the applicant agrees to it and the local planning authority consents to it. In addition, written representations are likely to be appropriate where there are disputes over factual matters.

There is also scope for an informal hearing in front of an inspector. The Planning Inspectorate may even suggest this to you.

An inquiry is a formal hearing, and the procedure is more strictly governed. These are public forums, both sides are very likely to have legal representations, and witnesses are likely to be called and cross-examined. Whether an oral appeal (at an inquiry or a hearing) or written representations are more appropriate will depend upon a series of factors, such as:

● The importance of the development.

● The amount of controversy it has generated.

● Its cost.

● The extent to which local residents have generated an interest in it.

The greater the local interest, the more likely that an oral hearing will be suggested. This is where it pays to keep your head low and not tell the entire village that you are proposing to knock down the "hundred-year-old barn that was used by the Smith family for four generations, and now you wish to build a big house with pool and sauna."

Whatever type of hearing is decided upon, there are certain hoops that the local planning authority will go through. For example, you can count on a site visit and other interested parties being notified – these parties may even receive copies of your appeal.

For both types of appeals you and your legal advisor need to prepare what is known in the trade as a "statement of case". This is where you present all your arguments, supported by evidence and cross-referred to legal precedents, existing legislation, planning guidance notes, development plans and anything else that you think will support your case. You also need to attach plans and photographs, and refer to any special circumstances that you feel are particular to your appeal. You should also consider giving reasons why you think that your plan would be beneficial to the environment and local community etc., particularly if the development may generate employment. This is the key document, so plan it well, structure your arguments clearly and concisely, and support each statement with facts and evidence.

If the hearing is a written one you need not do anything more until the decision is made. If it is an oral hearing (as opposed to an inquiry), it is likely to be informal and witnesses will be called to give evidence; normally, there is no cross-examination of the witnesses. If there is an inquiry, there are detailed rules about submissions of proofs of evidence and calling witnesses, who will be cross-examined by the council's legal representatives and also questioned by the inspector. The decision will be sent to you in writing, and the reasoning behind the decision will be set out.

Unlike legal proceedings, if you lose your appeal you are unlikely to have to pay the winning party's costs in defending the appeal. Conversely, if you win, there is little scope for you to recover your expenses from the local authority, unless it can be demonstrated that the authority acted unreasonably.

If the decision is unfavourable, there is recourse, in limited circumstances, to a review by the High Court.

SUMMARY

It is unfortunate that appeals are required for planning decisions, particularly when an applicant is appealing against the mere failure of the local authority to provide a decision. The time and expense incurred due to such administrative oversights can be significant, but that is the nature of the planning system. If it becomes apparent that you will appeal against the original planning decision, it may be worth considering handing the matter over to the lawyers, unless your case is so black and white that your are confident of getting the ball over the line unaided.

Enforcement of planning controls

A breach of a planning control is not necessarily a criminal offence. Indeed, planning controls can, in certain circumstances, be broken and then granted retrospectively. In some cases, the authority can even run out of time and be unable to bring an action if they notice the breach some years later. However, failure to comply with some of the notices discussed here can amount to a criminal offence, as can obstructing a planning officer in the carrying out of his duties. Here, we examine the enforcement action that the planning authority is entitled to take for a breach of a planning condition.

If the breach relates to a building or engineering operation, or if there was a change of use to a dwelling house, the time limit for the planning authority to take any action is four years from the date that the project was completed. In all other cases it is ten years. The planning authorities are not bound by these time limits where listed buildings are concerned.

When a local authority is contemplating enforcement action, it is usual practice for them to invite you to apply for retrospective planning permission. If retrospective planning permission is granted, the local authority cannot proceed with the enforcement. However, if the application is rejected they may commence enforcement proceedings.

The planning authority has the power to enter into your property at a reasonable hour for the purposes of investigating any breach of planning control, and to determine whether any enforcement action should be taken, or if it has been taken, whether it has been fully complied with.

These powers of entry are limited. The planning authority must have reasonable grounds for believing that there has been a breach of planning consent or non-compliance with an enforcement action. This power is further limited in the case of a dwelling house, where they are obliged to give you at least 24 hours notice of any proposed entry.

You can refuse entry, but if you do the planning authority is likely to procure a warrant from a magistrate authorising entry. A warrant can also be obtained if the planning authority reasonably believes that it will be refused entry, or if the case is urgent. It would also be unwise to be uncooperative should the planning authority exercise its power of entry. To obstruct a planning officer is a criminal offence.

This approach does seem heavy-handed, and fortunately it is not the preferred approach when the planning authority seeks to ascertain whether there has been a breach of the planning control.

Planning Contravention Notice

The planning authority normally sends out a Planning Contravention Notice (PCN), which sets out in detail what the alleged breach is and gives the person served an opportunity to respond. The PCN may be served on the owner or occupier of the land or anyone carrying out operations on that land. Once served with a PCN, you have 21 days to respond. A failure to respond, or knowingly or recklessly making a false statement in response to a PCN, is a criminal offence.

Injunctions

Another weapon in the arsenal of the planning authorities is an injunction. An injunction is an order issued by the court that requires the person against whom it is issued to stop the activities that are causing the breach of the planning control. It is an "equitable remedy", so the court has a discretion both to order the injunction and decide its terms.

Enforcement notice

If a planning condition is breached, you are unlikely to have committed a criminal offence. However, non-compliance with an enforcement notice which has been served in respect of a breach of planning control is a criminal offence.

The planning authority may issue an enforcement notice if it appears that there has been a breach of planning control and that an enforcement notice is the most expeditious way to deal with the breach. The notice must specify the breach, what steps must be taken and by when, as well as the date on which the enforcement notice becomes effective.

If the notice does not comply with these basic requirements, it may be void. The practical consequence of this is that it simply buys more time, as the planning authority will simply reissue the enforcement notice.

If you do not comply with the notice, not only is it a criminal offence, but the local planning authority may also enter onto your land and rectify the breach at your expense.

Once an enforcement notice has been issued, it does not become effective until 28 days after it has been served. The effect of the enforcement notice may also be suspended until any appeals have been dealt with. Therefore, in the interim, while any appeals are being heard, the planning authority may issue a stop notice.

Stop notice

The local planning authority may issue a stop notice to ensure that the activities that brought about the breach of planning control are brought to an end before the enforcement notice takes effect. However, if the activity to which the stop notice refers has been carried out for more than four years, or if it relates to the use of a building as a dwelling house, the stop notice is not effective. Unlike enforcement notices, there is no appeal against stop notices.

Breach of condition notice

A breach of condition notice is issued by the planning authority to ensure that some action is carried out to ensure compliance with the planning conditions or limitations (as opposed to restricting or stopping an activity). The notice will set out the steps that need to be taken to ensure compliance with the planning conditions, and the notice period within which the recipient must comply.

Appealing against an enforcement notice

It is possible to appeal against an enforcement notice, and listed below are some of the grounds upon which you can appeal: *(text continues on page 45)*

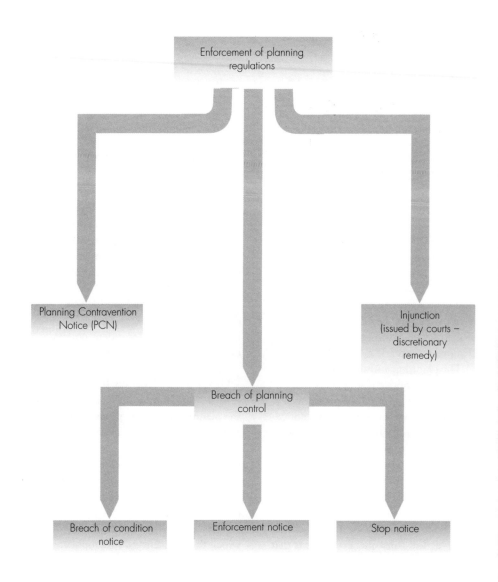

Enforcement notices.

● Planning permission ought to be granted.

● The conditions attached to the consent ought to be discharged.

● The matters alleged in the notice have not occurred, or if they have, they do not warrant an enforcement notice.

● Either the period required to cease activities or the steps that are required to be taken are unreasonable.

● The planning authority has served the notice incorrectly.

Any appeal must be lodged before the enforcement notice takes effect. It must also state the grounds of the appeal and be accompanied by the appropriate fee.

Compensation

In the event that a stop notice is issued and the enforcement notice is either quashed, varied (so that the activities are no longer prohibited), or withdrawn, compensation is payable to any person who has an interest in the land and has suffered a loss as a result.

SUMMARY

If you continue to act in contravention of a stop notice or an enforcement notice, you are carrying out a criminal offence. Breach of condition notices and stop notices cannot be appealed against. In relation to the breach of condition notice, it is a defence to show that the recipient took all reasonable steps to ensure compliance with the notice, or that the recipient did not have control of the land at the time the notice was served. If you are successful in your appeal, you are entitled to compensation. Enforcement notices can be appealed against. Finally, the court may issue an injunction if a notice would not be effective in stopping the breach.

A failure to comply with either a stop notice or an enforcement notice may result in a fine of a maximum of £20,000 (at the time of writing). If it is an indictment (Crown Court hearing), the fine is limitless. In making a fine the courts may also factor in any financial benefits that may have been obtained during the breach – for example, profits made while a bed and breakfast was being operated in contravention of either a stop notice or an enforcement notice.

Conservation Areas

Building in Conservation Areas, National Parks and even Areas Of Outstanding Natural Beauty brings a new dimension to the planning restrictions that have already been set out. The reason for this is simple – to preserve the unique character of the area.

The exceptions to a "development" that were set out earlier will not necessarily apply to Conservation Areas. The laws that deal with Conservation Areas are set out in the Planning (Listed Buildings and Conservation Areas) Act 1990. Part ii deals with Conservation Areas.

The crux when developing in a Conservation Area is to ensure that whatever you submit, you will pay special attention to preserving or even enhancing the character of the area. This is the key test that will be applied by the relevant authority.

A common misconception made by home builders and improvers is that a building needs to be listed in order for it to be subject to additional planning restrictions. This is not the case. The building merely needs to be located in a Conservation Area to be subject to the additional restrictions.

You are likely to require additional Conservation Area consent where you are carrying out works to a house located in the Conservation Area, for example:

● If you intend on demolishing a building or a significant part of it.

● It is an open question whether the demolition of the internal parts of a building would require special

consent. It is my opinion that this is generally not the case, and that such minor internal works would be alterations and subject only to the normal planning requirements.

Conservation Area consent is unlikely to be required for:

● Minor external work that would not amount to development (and therefore not requiring planning consent).

● Constructing a new building in a Conservation Area (but planning consent is required).

Submitting an application for Conservation Area consent

The applications for Conservation Area consent and listed building consent are very similar. You make the application to the appropriate local authority – some local authorities use the same form whether you are applying for listed buildings consent or Conservation Area consent.

Once the authority gets your application, they consider it and advertise a notice in the local press. This is where things get interesting. Sod's law ensures that a collection of objectors will see the advertisement and then make all sorts of representations to the authority in an attempt to restrict the development. This is where it pays dividends to consult your neighbours and take into account their thoughts – just consulting them may be sufficient to ward off countless objections that may destroy your plans.

The time within which the local authority has to make a decision on your

Dead or dying trees.

A tree that has a diameter of less than 75 mm at 1.5 m above ground level.

application and your rights of appeal is the same as for listed buildings. All Conservation Area consents last for five years, unless they state otherwise. As with planning consent, Conservation Area consent can be given subject to certain conditions.

As with listed buildings, you must carefully consider your actions if you are developing in a Conservation Area, as some activities (unlike normal planning consents) may be criminal activities if you do not have the appropriate Conservation Area consent in place.

Applications for Conservation Area consent are not limited to works to existing buildings. You may also need to make an application to the local authority if you intend to cut down a tree.

In the beginning of this section I set out that the overriding principle of local authorities when considering Conservation Area consents is the maintenance of the character of the area, or the enhancement of it. Trees, hedges, gardens and the like are critical elements of any such environment, so you may need to get separate consent if you plan on taking down a tree, because by taking it down you may generate a negative impact on the Conservation Area. There are exceptions. For example, if the tree is:

● Dead or dying.

● In diameter less than 75 mm at 1.5 m above ground level.

Trees that are a hazard or a nuisance.

● A hazard or a nuisance.

Tree Preservation Orders

A Tree Preservation Order (TPO) protects a tree or group of trees in addition to those protective rights set out previously. Trees may need to be protected in order to conserve the nature of an area. If a TPO is in place, you should know about it as a consequence of the searches that your solicitor has carried out prior to you purchasing the site. Lawyers have great fun in trying to ascertain what exactly is a tree – in 1826 it was decided that a tree was "wood applicable to buildings and does not include orchard trees". The size of a tree is not definitive of what is a tree, as a TPO may be in place with respect to

saplings. The best advice would be to use your common sense and contact the local authority.

Why are TPOs of interest to us? Put simply, it is a criminal offence to carry out works to a tree that is the subject of a TPO unless you have the local authority's consent, and the best bit is that it is no defence if you shrug your shoulders and say you never knew about the TPO.

Listed buildings

Listed buildings is a generic term. There are different classes (or grades) of listed buildings. The logic of some of the classifications does verge on the banal, but the overriding logic of preserving a historical building is sound enough.

You may need to consider the provisions peculiar to listed buildings even if you are only carrying out works with the area of land associated with a building that is listed. If it is decided that your building is to be listed, there is little you can practically do about it. You can get wind of whether a planning authority is proposing to "list" a building by making enquiries with both local residents and the local authority. A tell-tale sign is if the property has a building preservation notice attached to it.

It is a criminal offence to alter a listed building in a manner which alters its character or historical integrity; as with Conservation Areas, it is no defence to plead ignorance.

An application for listed buildings consent is made to the appropriate authority, and the consent (if given) to carry out works to the premises is likely to have conditions attached to it – just like normal planning consents. If you are not happy with the conditions you can go back to the local authority to have the conditions varied or even discharged.

When building an extension to a property, careful consideration must be given where the adjoining wall of the extension meets the listed building. Local authorities have extensive powers to restrain activities that have been carried out without consent, to the extent that in addition to the criminal offence committed, the owner may need to reinstate the building to its former state. There is no time limit within which the authority need bring an action for unauthorised works.

There are limited defences for unauthorised works to listed buildings. These are if the works were urgent for reasons of health and safety, or to preserve the building's integrity; and:

● The works were limited to the minimum amount necessary.

● The works affording temporary support or shelter were not possible.

● Written notification given to the local planning authority as soon as practicable.

Grades of Listed Buildings

GRADE I	GRADE II	GRADE II*	GRADE III
Buildings of special interest.	Important buildings that are more than just of special interest.	Buildings of exceptionally special interest to which every effort is made to preserve them.	This grade is no longer used. Such buildings are usually reclassified as Grade II.

Case Study

Daniel and Katy were planning a family, and had spotted their dream house. The terraced house was a far cry from what they considered to be a listed building. They instructed lawyers, put their flat up for sale, and got the surveyors round. It was not until fairly late in the transaction that it transpired that the building (which was listed) had had some fairly extensive works done to it, and consent had never been obtained. These works were carried out ten years ago, so it was tempting for Daniel to take the view that even though the works to the building did not have listed building consent, and the works had been carried such a long time ago, who would know? Unfortunately, to proceed with the purchase would have placed Daniel and Katy in a precarious position. They might have had to reinstate the premises, and they might have had problems reselling the building. Most crucially of all, no mortgage lender would have lent them the money to complete the purchase, as the risk would have been unacceptable. In addition to this, no Building Regulations approval was ever given for the works.

KEY POINTS

● Are you carrying out a development? If yes, you may need planning consent.

● Does the development fall within an exemption? If so, planning consent may not need to be applied for.

● If no planning consent is required, consider whether there are any Article 4 orders (etc.) in force.

● Is it a listed building, or is the property in a Conservation Area? If so, consider separate listed building and Conservation Area consents.

● It is an offence to:
  ✎ breach an enforcement notice.
  ✎ breach a stop notice.
  ✎ obstruct a planning officer.
  ✎ carry out works to a listed building without consent.
  ✎ carry out works to a building in a Conservation Area without consent.
  ✎ carry out works to trees that are subject to Tree Preservation Orders.

Archaeological finds

Great Britain is a country steeped in a rich history dating back to the Stone Age. Many developments throw up new archaeological finds, and in a perverse way, the process of building has enabled us to uncover more of the country's history than leaving the land untouched. It is a distinct possibility that your plot or extension will throw up some archaeological wonders. The first port of call is English Heritage, who take a pragmatic approach to each archaeological find that is of interest.

Before you start your development (or even purchase the plot of land), you should contact your county council who have a record of the county's sites and monuments – usually referred to as an SMR. The SMR will flag up any archaeological remains close to or within the actual area you are going to develop. You could also consult the development plan of the local authority for your locality.

The contents of the SMR or the development plan may have an impact on your project. If it seems as though there may be items of archaeological interest the local authority may request that you carry out an archaeological investigation of the site. This investigation will involve the services of an archaeologist together with a physical survey of the site.

If archaeological finds are likely, the next step is to determine the strategy to adopt in order to preserve any such finds. The key factor is preservation. This could mean leaving the archaeological finds underground, as this may be the best method of preserving them.

The manner in which any artefacts are dealt with may also form the obligations in a Section 106 agreement. You may even get funding from English Heritage to pay for any excavations.

In addition to English Heritage, other useful organisations are:

● The Council for British Archaeology.

● The Institute of Field Archaeologists.

Building Regulations

Every building project, whether it is a new build or simple internal non-structural alterations, will need to comply with the current Building Regulations. Compliance will need to be signed off by the building control officer or district surveyor of your local authority. It is possible that some local authorities will accept NHBC Buildmark cover as evidence of compliance with building regulations. Building regulations are there to ensure that the works will be, and have been, carried out in a safe manner, using suitable materials.

If you sell your property, it is very likely that a purchaser will insist on a certificate from the local authority evidencing that the works comply with the Building Regulations. Building Regulations are separate from planning consents, and you will need to obtain consents for both.

The current Building Regulations came into force in 1992 and are frequently updated as new safety issues arise. When you submit your building plans, the local authority will usually approve them unless the plans are going to breach the Building Regulations.

The building control officer may suggest alterations and will attend site every so often to ensure that the works are being carried out in accordance with the current Building Regulations. While it is a condition of most standard building contracts that the contractor carries out the works in accordance with the Building Regulations, it would be prudent to check that this is/was the case and not have to rely on pursuing the contractor for a breach of contract if it was found that his works were not in accordance with the regulations. If you do not have a formal (written) building contract, it is likely that the courts will imply that the contract would have required the builder to comply with the building regulations when carrying out the works.

If you fail to comply with the Building Regulations, not only will you have difficulties in selling your property, you may also find yourself at risk of criminal prosecution.

If you are found to be contravening the Building Regulations, you may be (at current levels) fined up to £5,000 for each offence and a further £50 a day for each day that the offence continues.

CHAPTER 4

Environmental Law for Home Improvers and Builders

Environmental issues are an important part of buying and developing a plot of land. It might be that the searches on your plot have uncovered some environmental concerns, or you are planning on constructing an environmentally friendly house. Environmental issues are likely to hit you financially rather than in the traditional, legal sense. This chapter introduces the key aspects of some environmental regulations that may affect you.

Regulatory bodies

The key bodies that you may get involved with are your local authority and the Environment Agency.

The appropriate local authority is responsible for identifying and overseeing the clearing up of contaminated land and for taking action in respect of anything that might be a nuisance to the general public (statutory nuisance). Generally speaking, the local authority will not clear up environmental pollutants if they are on private land, but they will assist you by giving you names of suitable companies to help you clean up the pollutants. Your local authority is also likely to take a hands-off approach to contaminated land, in that it is likely to let market forces ensure the clean-up of contaminated land (unless the contamination is significant).

The Environment Agency oversees the implementation of the environmental regulations. It has the power to give authorisations, serve prohibition notices and prosecute offenders. It also regulates the waste management licences that may be of interest to some house builders.

Finally, the privatised water industries have the power to prosecute parties who (amongst other offences) either pollute the sewage systems or breach the terms of their licence for discharge into the sewers.

General responsibility

"The polluter pays." This is the mantra of environmental legislation in England and Wales. The polluter includes someone who causes or "knowingly permits" the contamination. You may also be liable where you learn about contamination but do nothing to stop it. However, if the original polluter cannot be found, the risk of cleaning up the land may rest with you, as the owner of a contaminated site. It is possible to transfer the liability for contaminated land from the seller to a purchaser at the time of the sale. This will be determined by factors such as the purchaser's knowledge at the time of the sale. If the buyer is aware at the time of the sale of the environmental state of the site, he may be deemed to accept a transfer of liability from the seller. This may also be reflected in a reduced purchase price, and for the sake of clarity, this is often documented in the sale documentation.

If you have concerns as to the location or history of your plot, it is advisable to ensure that an environmental search is carried out before you exchange contracts on your purchase by one of the many companies that undertake these searches at a reasonable price. Your solicitor or legal advisor will advise you if they feel such a search is necessary.

Contaminated land

The risk in buying land that is contaminated can be immense, as you could face both civil and criminal liabilities. However, unless the plot is significantly contaminated, you are unlikely to deal with such issues. Your local authority should have a register of significantly contaminated sites, although this is unlikely to be comprehensive.

The safest way of finding out if your land is contaminated is to ensure that your solicitor carries out an environmental search against the property on your behalf. This type of search is becoming more common in conveyancing transactions. On the basis of an initial survey, you can decide if a more detailed survey should be carried out. The detailed survey will ascertain the type (if any) of the contaminants, and should also price the clean-up costs.

One thing that you should keep your eye on is the limitation of liability that the environmental search company is prepared to cover itself for. Many companies limit their liability to a measly £250,000 – this amount is clearly unsatisfactory at today's house prices, and will not cover your potential losses in capital value and clean-up costs if pollutants are found and the environmental search company is found to be negligent.

Buying and selling contaminated land

If the seller (the person who caused or knows that the land is contaminated) provides to the buyer information as to the contamination of the land when it is purchased, he may be excluded from any clean-up liabilities (known as remediation liabilities).

The most common way of dealing with contaminated land in residential plot purchases is for the seller to reduce the sale price by an appropriate amount relative to the clean-up cost. The onus will then be on the buyer to meet any remediation costs.

However, it is possible for a buyer to enter into an agreement with the seller agreeing which party is responsible for the contaminated land. The sale could also be made conditional upon the site being remediated, or a pot of money could be set aside on the sale for the remediation works, with any excess being returned to the seller. It is also possible to limit your liability for remediation costs with suitable insurance cover.

It is for the local authority to determine whether the land is contaminated. As the occupier of a plot, you are not obligated to notify your local authority of your suspicions that the land may be contaminated. However, an owner would not be entitled to any reduction in the cost of clean-up that may be offered by the local authority if they knew that the land was contaminated, failed to decontaminate it (within reason), and chose not to inform the local authority.

If you are borrowing money to buy the site and the site is contaminated, your mortgage lender is likely to want to protect its position. This is because the lender is at risk for clean-up costs and is exposed to criminal liabilities. For example, if you buy the land and for some reason the lender has to repossess it, then the risk of clean-up costs rests with them. In practical terms, this means additional environmental assessments will be carried out in order to satisfy the lender.

Planning applications and environmental legislation

The local authority will consider the environmental impact of your proposed development when considering your planning application, and will possibly make planning conditional on environmental issues being satisfactorily dealt with. This is in addition to scrutinising your proposed plan in the context of their planning policies.

If these issues are a concern, I suggest you discuss your proposals with the council's planning officer. You can obtain the appropriate Planning Guidance Notes from HM Stationery Office or download them from the Internet.

For homebuilders who plan to construct an environmentally friendly house, an examination of the Department of the Environment's guidance notes on waste management and a discussion with the Environment Agency and the planning department of the local authority is advisable.

Waste management

The management of waste depends principally upon whether or not the waste that you are dealing with is regarded as being "controlled waste". You can find out if this is the case by looking it up in the annex to the Waste Management Licensing Regulations – the internet link to this regulation is listed on page 170. If the waste is controlled and you intend to discard it, you may require a waste management licence. This may concern you if you are demolishing an existing building or if you are constructing your house in line with the concept of sustainable development.

The average home builder is unlikely to require a licence if the waste is put to some beneficial use or is regarded as being domestic waste. Temporary waste storage (such as a skip) does not require a waste management licence. However, a separate licence will be required if the skip is left on the highway. For further information on these points contact the Waste Policy Division of the Environment Agency.

Statutory nuisance

Statutory nuisances are also the domain of the local authority. Examples of what the local authority may prosecute landowners for are:

● Land that is kept in a state that is prejudicial to health.

● Emissions that are prejudicial to health, such as dust, smoke and smells.

● Noise that is prejudicial to health or a nuisance.

The local authority deals with such nuisances by issuing an abatement notice on the "appropriate person". The abatement notice sets out the steps that need to be taken to stop the nuisance. If you consider that a statutory nuisance is occurring, your first port of call is to inform the environmental team at your local authority. The person on whom the abatement notice is served has 21 days to appeal against it.

The "appropriate person" is, in the first instance, the person who caused or is causing the nuisance. If this person cannot be found, the next "appropriate person" is the owner or occupier of the land. It is a defence to show that the person had used best practicable means to prevent or minimise the nuisance. It is possible for an individual to bring an action in a magistrates court for a statutory nuisance. The court may then issue an abatement notice. Failure to comply with an abatement notice is a criminal offence.

Water pollution

A common offence committed by home builders when building extensions is to confuse the drainage pipes and the sewage pipes. The two systems are separate from each other: rainwater goes untreated into rivers and streams (which back on to people's gardens and village greens), while sewage goes through a separate system to be treated. If you mix these pipes up – which is easily done – you have raw sewage going into villages, brooks and streams, causing untold environmental damage, particularly if the brook or stream overflows. Needless to say, such a mistake is an offence.

There is no defence for such an offence. You need only cause or knowingly permit the pollution of controlled waters in order to be at risk of a criminal prosecution. The courts have defined the act of "knowingly permitting" very widely. Turning a blind eye or refraining from making an enquiry would be enough to land you in court.

You are not absolved from any criminal liabilities if you have recently purchased a property that is polluting controlled waters – simply allowing the pollution to continue is sufficient to land you in court.

Courts can fine you (at current levels) up to £20,000 for each offence or six months in prison. If the case is heard in the Crown Court, the fine is limitless.

Enforcement

Each of the government bodies that were introduced at the beginning of this chapter has a separate responsibility for different aspects of environmental enforcement. The bodies that concern the average house builder are:

● The Environment Agency, which regulates waste and water offences.

● The local authority, which prosecutes statutory nuisances and requires the clean-up of contaminated land.

● Private water companies, which prosecute for sewerage offences.

In relation to plots that are contaminated, it may be that a remediation notice has been (or may be) issued upon whomever the local authority regard as being the "appropriate person", even if this person may be entirely innocent of causing any pollution. The remediation notice will set out what needs to be done to stop the contamination and what clean-up must be carried out on the land.

It is very unlikely that a remediation notice is received without any warning. Local authorities tend to go through an extensive period of consultation with the landowner/polluter before issuing any such notice.

Remediation notices can be appealed against within 21 days of being issued. Unless you have a reasonable excuse, failure to comply with a remediation notice is a criminal offence. Continuing failure is likely to result in the local authority carrying out the remediation works and seeking to recover these costs from the "appropriate person".

KEY POINTS

- Give careful consideration to any environmental risks that may be associated with that plot – a lot of information can be obtained from the local authority's records and the previous use of the site. The biggest impact of any environmental concerns will be cost.

- Be wary if you know or suspect of some previous activity having been carried out to the plot that may give rise to environmental concerns.

- Even if you did not cause the pollution, you may still be responsible for the clean-up costs.

- Unlike planning conditions, breaches of remediation notices and abatement notices as well as other aspects of environmental legislation (pollution of controlled waters), are criminal offences.

CHAPTER 5

Planning the Construction Works

This chapter will trigger questions that you should be asking yourself before you contemplate beginning any construction works. It assumes that you already have planning consent (if required). The aim is that by the end of the chapter you have planned out who is going to carry out what works – design or physical – and when the works will be completed.

Undertaking a new build or an extension to an existing home can be an immense undertaking – not only in terms of the financial aspects, legal and building practicalities, but in respect of stresses on family life. A new build may require you to live on site in a caravan for between six months and a year, while an extension can cause upheaval to normal family life, with tradesmen coming and going, noise, dust and other numerous headaches. You will need to give this careful thought,

consult your family and ensure that they are on board for all eventualities.

Allocating responsibilities

Before any trip to the builder's merchants, plan each aspect of the construction phase of your project. You may decide that you are going to design and build the entire project yourself, but it is more likely that you will allocate the specialist tasks to suitable professionals. The roles of these professionals are shown in the box below.

Step One: mortgage lender requirements

If your house is mortgaged, you should consider what provisions are contained in your mortgage documents relating to proposed construction works at the property. Mortgage lenders can get very

PROFESSIONAL	ROLE
Architect	Prepares the plans for the overall design of the project. Can also manage the entire project.
Structural engineer	Works on the architect's plans to ensure that the building will be structurally safe.
Mechanical and services engineer	Designs the services. These are things like optic cables, information technology integration, air-conditioning and heating units.
Planning supervisor	Ensures a safe construction site.
Quantity surveyor	Prepares the bills of quantity, which price each element of the project.

nervous when they learn that construction works are being carried out on their security for their loan. The requirements that they tend to have are that the professional team is both insured (and their insurance is both sufficient and up-to-date for the project) and that each individual member belongs to an accepted professional organisation: architects should be members of the RIBA (Royal Institute of British Architects), engineers the ACE (Association of Consulting Engineers), and quantity surveyors the RICS (Royal Institution of Charted Surveyors). Each of these professional bodies produces a formal appointment documenting the relationship in the form of a contract between yourself and the professional.

The lender many also insist that the new build has NHBC or Zurich cover, which are considered later in this chapter.

Step Two: who prepares the designs?

In general, there are two options; instructing individual professionals to prepare the designs on your behalf and then appointing a contractor to carry out the works, or getting a design-and-build contractor to prepare the designs and build the development.

If you instruct architects and structural engineers to prepare the plans on your behalf, you tend to have a greater input in the design process. These plans will then be collated to form a part of the tender that is sent out to several contractors, who prepare a quote based on these drawings and associated documentation (like the bills of quantity). I refer to this option as the "traditional method".

The second option is to instruct a design-and-build contractor to carry out both the design and construction of the entire project. Design and build is like a one-stop shop for your project.

There are advantages and disadvantages with each option. Having separate designers and contractors can cause difficulty when allocating responsibility for defective workmanship. For example, if you have a leaking roof you will need to ascertain whether this leak is caused by a defective design or defective workmanship. If it is defective design, your claim is against the designer, but if the builder did not build the roof in accordance with the designs, the claim is against him. The traditional method also requires you to give careful thought as to which party is responsible for various tasks and who is responsible for obtaining planning consent. Having a contractor who is responsible for both the design and build of the project provides single-point responsibility for any claims. It also takes a significant workload off your shoulders. The design-and-build contractor should be responsible for making all requisite planning applications (as ever, you will need to check the terms of the contract to ensure this is the case).

Design and build

Instructing a contractor to carry out both the design and build of your project is relatively straightforward. In practice, you approach a design-and-build contractor with your proposals and they prepare the plans and quote you a fee for the entire job.

I would not advise using a design-and-build contractor for jobs that have complex design elements. Design-and-build contractors have a set design and programme that they work to – for example, many of the companies that advertise in the national Sunday press for the construction of a conservatory are illustrative of small-scale design-and-build contractors.

Design-and-build contractors have set designs and materials and work to a pre-determined programme of works. In many cases their materials are pre-fabricated offsite and incorporated into the extension/conservatory/shed etc. that they advertise to build.

Design and build contractual relationship.

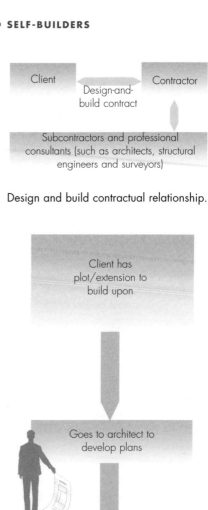

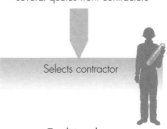

Design and build.

Traditional.

Traditional

This is a generic term and is the most likely procurement method that you will use, as it is also the most flexible. With this method you can pick and choose which elements you want to outsource and which you want to carry out yourself; the concept is applicable to both the design and construction elements of your project.

At its core it involves approaching a designer who then draws up the plans, usually just outline drawings. The next step is usually to get the planning consent based on these outline plans (it is unwise to purchase a plot without having at least outline planning consent in place). Once consent has been obtained, the architect will prepare full plans. You can also employ a quantity surveyor to price the works. Once the plans and the bills are prepared you should get several quotes from various contractors for the works.

Before going to tender, consider whether you are you going to carry out all the physical work or only the non-specialist elements, leaving things such as piling to specialist contractors. You can then get individual quotes for each element as you go. Another option is for you to carry out a project-management role and get the contractor to complete all the works.

Consider each quote (tender) with your architect and quantity surveyor. You should not focus just on the figure – the

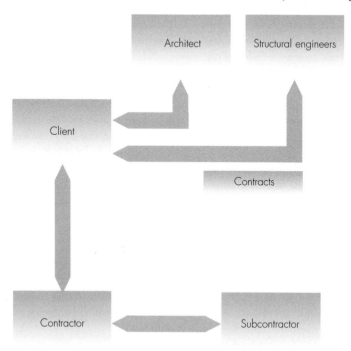

Traditional contractual relationship.

method of construction is equally important. A suspiciously cheap price will only cause problems later on, and conversely an excessive quote may simply be overcautious. Also consider whether the contractors are overpricing certain elements of the works, requesting an advance payment, or front-loading their quote (so that they get a disproportionate amount of money early on in the project). These practices should ring alarm bells.

Step Three: insurance

There are three types of insurance cover that you will encounter:

● **Professional indemnity insurance** – this covers negligent design, and must be held by the architect, structural engineer, design-and-build contractor and any other designer employed on the project.

● **Public liability insurance** – this covers any instance of the works injuring a third party.

● **Contractor's all-risks insurance** – this insurance covers "all risks", but is usually limited to the risks listed in the policy.

I advise you to read the insurance documents (usually only a single sheet of paper) to ensure that the cover:

● Is sufficient – keep an eye out for policies where sums are capped in the aggregate, and not for each and every claim.

● Is in force.

● Has no unacceptable exclusions.

Warranty cover

Many lenders insist on some form of warranty cover for a newly built home. Having a warranty in place from either the NHBC, Zurich or Premier Warranty greatly enhances the marketability of your home. It is essential that you have one in place if you intend on reselling your home within ten years as without one you are likely to face difficulties in selling your self-built home. Few buyers will be able to obtain a mortgage to buy your home without such a guarantee.

NHBC and Zurich are the two main warranty providers. Both have different products available, depending upon the scope of your project.

NHBC have two products that are of interest to self-builders and home improvers – the Solo and Buildmark schemes. Solo is designed for self builders who take a hands-on role in building their own home, in that they buy materials and carry out some of the building work themselves and/or employ subcontractors to carry out the specialist works.

The Buildmark cover is the NHBC's standard ten-year protection. Here, you would need to employ an NHBC-approved contractor.

Zurich has two products that compete directly with the NHBC – Custom Build for self-builders (similar to Solo), and New Build, which competes with Buildmark.

Both companies offer broadly the same cover for 10–12 years, and should also cover you for the insolvency of the main contractor. There is a premium for this cover, typically in the region of £1,500. They also have their own checking requirements before the guarantee is issued.

The cover is not comprehensive, and there are many alleged stories in the national press where self-builders have been caught out by obscure provisions in the policies preventing them from relying on the cover that they thought they had – so read the small print! You may feel that a warranty is both a waste of effort and money, but if you are planning on selling your home within 10–12 years of its completion, you may find it almost impossible to sell without such a warranty in place.

VAT

When planning the finances of your project, you should consider some of the VAT (Value Added Tax) tax breaks that may be on offer to home builders, particularly if the new building or conversion will have some charitable usage. In-depth consideration of VAT is outside the scope of this book, but the aim is to get you thinking about tax breaks that may apply to you. Contact Customs and Excise or an accountant for more information on VAT. VAT is generally "charged on any supply of goods or services made in the United Kingdom where it is a taxable supply made by a taxable person in the course or furtherance of any business carried on by him" (Value Added Tax Act 1994 s(4)1) – the tax is charged on the value of the supply.

Zero-rated projects

The construction of a new dwelling or a number of dwellings is zero-rated. So is the construction of a building intended for use as a relevant residential or charitable purpose. The definition of "dwelling" includes a garage that is constructed at the same time as the dwelling for occupation (together with it). The supply of materials used for such projects is also zero-rated. You cannot zero-rate all materials: for example, things like prefabricated furniture (unless it is for your kitchen), carpets and domestic gas and electrical appliances (unless they are for space or water heating) are not zero-rated. The services of your professional team (architects, surveyors and other consultants) are also not zero-rated, nor is the conversion, reconstruction, alteration or enlargement of an existing building.

Substantial alterations (not maintenance or repair works) to the fabric of listed buildings that are used for a residential or charitable purpose are zero-rated – this includes works to the floor, walls, ceilings etc.

Reduced VAT

Reduced VAT (five per cent at time of writing) is payable on the following:

- Converting non-residential property into a care home or bedsits.

- Renovating a care home or bed sit that has been empty for three years.

- The construction, renovation or conversion of a building into a garage as part of a larger reduced rate project.

SUMMARY OF VAT (Source: HM Customs and Excise VAT Notice 708)		
Works	Rate of VAT on construction	Rate of VAT on professional services
New build of residential dwellings	Zero	17.5%
Alterations, refurbishment and repairs	17.5%	17.5%
Alterations to a listed building	Zero	17.5%
Repairs and maintenance to a listed building	17.5%	17.5%
Converting a non-residential premises to a dwelling	5%	17.5%
Renovations to a house that has been empty for three–ten years	5%	17.5%

The law on VAT is constantly changing, and I suggest you seek up-to-date professional tax advice.

Tendering

Once you have decided on how you are going to manage your project and the extent to which you are going to use external contractors, it is time to put your proposals out to tender to ensure that you get the best available deal.

There are many different forms of

Case Study

Anna and Eric purchased an idyllic plot of land with an existing building on it that needed to be demolished. After a couple of months they got their planning application and began to do their sums. When considering their VAT position, they looked at: demolishing the existing home; building a new home with a detached garage; and building a swimming pool adjacent to the house. As the house is being built for residential purposes it would be zero-rated, as would the garage – provided it was built at the same time as the house and for use together with the house. However, Customs and Excise are likely to decide that the swimming pool is standard-rated. The swimming pool is not considered a dwelling; however, if the pool was attached to the house some accountants may argue that the cost of building the pool should be zero-rated!

tendering processes employed in the construction industry. The complexity of the process adopted will depend upon the individual project. For example; if you are going to carry out the bulk of the works, the tendering process may be as simple as emailing or calling a selection of specialist subcontractors to bid for specialist works such as piling. Alternatively, you may decide to take on a project-management role for the construction of your house, in which case your tendering process will take on a more formal structure.

A tender is simply an invitation to different contractors to make an offer on your proposal. Most developers accept the lowest price bidder, but this should not be the only consideration; you should have regard to the construction methods, manpower and materials to be employed.

KEY POINTS

- Think carefully about your involvement in the project. Will you prepare the plans and do the work yourself, or will you go to the other extreme and employ a design-and-build contractor to carry out your proposal?

- You may be entitled to tax breaks on the construction works – consult an accountant.

- If there is a remote chance that you may wish to sell your home within 12 years of its completion, I strongly recommend procuring warranty cover before you commence building works.

Irrespective of the tendering method that you use, you should be certain in your own mind what you want to achieve, as subsequent changes may prove expensive. You should also provide the bidders with as much relevant information as possible, to enable them to prepare an accurate bid.

Tender documents are traditionally made up of:

● Specifications.

● Bills of quantities.

● Contract drawing/plans.

● Draft form of building contract (with any proposed amendments).

● Form of tender.

When considering the tenders, do not focus only on the bottom price. Consider:

● The construction methods and materials employed, in case you have not specified these.

● The time frame for the works.

● The reputation of the bidding company.

Steps for safe selection

You may decide that your project does not warrant going through either a formal or informal tendering process. However, whatever type of contractor or subcontractor you do decide to employ, you must do your homework and ensure that they are not going to sit around site all day drinking tea, or at worst, disappearing with your cash. This checklist should also apply to each professional that you employ.

● Is the professional or construction company known to you? Were they recommended by friends or family?

● Have you seen any of their previous work? Do they have references?

● Is their field of expertise in a field that is similar in size, scope and complexity to your project?

Types of Tender Process

TWO-STAGE TENDERING	SELECTIVE TENDERING
Stage 1: approximately six bidders give a general price for the work.	The bid is sent out for tendering to between two–six contractors. All must be given exactly the same information in order to price their bid. This is the most common form of tendering.
Stage 2: more in-depth negotiations are developed with one or two contractors.	

● Are they affiliated to a professional organisation? If so, is their membership up to date?

● Do they carry insurance? If so, is this insurance up to date and sufficient to cover your potential losses (insurance cover should be sufficient to cover an entire rebuild plus 15 per cent for professional costs)?

● Are they a company? If so, do a company check at Companies House. This check is inexpensive and will:
  ✎ ensure that the company is not insolvent.
  ✎ show how long the company has been trading for.
  ✎ provide current profit-and-loss accounts and balance sheets.

● Are they VAT-registered? Rogue traders are rarely VAT-registered.

● A phone call to your local Trading Standards Council may shed some light on the shiftiest characters in the industry.

Consider asking for a performance bond from the contractor's bank or insurer. Depending upon the wording of the bond, it should cover you for the failure of the contractor to complete the contract, and should also cover your costs if he becomes insolvent.

KEY POINTS

● Prepare the tender documents with the assistance of your professional team.

● Before you send out the documents to tender, you must decide which party is doing what works; your role; your available budget; the scope of your project; and the time frame.

● A tender is an invitation for the contractors to make you an offer. There is no contract in place unless and until you accept this offer. You can accept an offer verbally, in writing or by your actions.

● Research the contractors' and professionals' backgrounds, and check their insurance, references and membership of professional bodies.

CHAPTER 6

Professional Appointments and Construction Contracts

This chapter is an introduction to professional appointments and the most common types of construction contracts that are available on the market. You should decide on the form of building contract that you propose to use before you send the drawings out to tender. The building contractor will price his tender against the works that need to be carried out and the contractual risks that he is exposing himself to under the building contract.

Appointing a professional team

Each of the professional institutions that your respective professional is likely to be a member of produces its own form of professional appointment. As the appointment is prepared by the body that the professional is a member of, the forms of appointment tend to be biased towards the professionals. RIBA, ACE and RICS produce several appointments, some of which are suited to smaller self-build projects. The forms of appointment come with guidance notes to help you complete them. There are different forms of appointment, depending upon whether you are going down the traditional procurement route or the design-and-build route.

In most self-build projects the professional tends to get appointed on the basis of a letter and an agreement of the fees. This is not satisfactory.

The key provisions that any appointment of a professional must have are:

● The standard of care that the professional must employ when carrying out the services on your behalf. The standard should be to that of a reasonable architect or similar professional skilled in carrying out services for projects of a similar size, scale and complexity as your project.

● An obligation to maintain professional indemnity cover for the duration of the contract, this being either 6 or 12 years.

● A copyright licence in your favour. This would entitle you to use all the drawings for any purpose associated with the project. The actual copyright remains with the professional, he is simply giving you a licence to use it. The professional should not qualify this copyright licence upon getting his fees. This is a qualification that you will find in the RIBA and ACE forms of appointment and should, in my opinion, be deleted.

● An obligation not to specify for use (or to use reasonable skill and care to bring to your attention the use of) any deleterious material. What materials are deleterious are open to discussion, as many materials (such as calcium silicate) are not deleterious in themselves but may be deleterious depending upon the manner in which they are used. An acceptable catch-all is to require that all materials satisfy the essential requirements laid down in the Construction Products Regulations 1991.

● How much the consultant is to be paid for the services, and by when. The appointment should also specify what rate the consultant is entitled to for any additional services, and whether disbursements are included in the fee. Professionals tend to charge a percentage of the total construction cost as their fee. A ballpark figure is three–seven per cent of the total construction cost, depending upon the scope and complexity of the works.

● What services the consultant is to employ. This is critical, as you can be sure that if the services are not listed in the appointment and you ask the consultant to carry out these additional services, they are going to ask for more money. You will also need to be careful that there is no overlapping of services: for example, drainage works can be the responsibility of either the architect or structural engineer.

● A valid execution clause. If the appointment is to be signed by an individual, it will need to be witnessed. If the consultant is a partnership, each partner must sign and the signatures witnessed. If it is a company, the appointment must be signed by both a director of the company and either a second company director or the company secretary.

● Keep your eye out for any clauses that limit the consultant's liability for defective works. Some consultants cap their liability at a certain figure by stating something along the lines of "the consultant's liability under this agreement shall not exceed £X". If there is a financial cap on the consultant's liability, consider whether this figure is sufficient to cover your potential losses.

Standard forms of building contract

There are many published standard forms of building contracts. The most common are the range of contracts produced by the Joint Contracts Tribunal (JCT), which range from simple contracts such as the JCT Building Contract for Homeowners and Occupiers 1999 to the complex JCT Standard Form of Building Contract 1998. These contracts are bought off the shelf and are available from most building bookshops and building organisations. Engineering contractors use the ICE (Institute of Civil Engineers) form of engineering contracts, which are outside the scope of this book.

Some contractors may propose their own form of contract – build-and-design contractors typically offer their own form of contract with reams of small print. If you are faced with the visual splendour of the deceptive small print, I suggest proposing to the contractor one of the standard forms discussed in this chapter. They can have no grounds to resist, as these forms are the industry standard.

It is not uncommon for the contractual provisions of the standard forms to be amended. If these amendments are lengthy, or if you do not understand what is being proposed, seek professional advice.

For the purposes of this book I have focused on the JCT forms of building contract, as these are the most common forms of contract that you will be offered or should propose to the contractor.

JCT Building Contract for Homeowners and Occupiers 1999

This is the most straightforward, standard form of building contract available. It is designed with independent homeowners in mind, is devoid of legal jargon and has been awarded a Crystal Mark for clarity in its use of English. It also has extensive guidance notes. The trick with this contract is to ensure that you know exactly what the scope of the works are. The JCT maintain that the contract is ideal for home improvements, repairs and extensions.

The contract allows the employer to withhold five per cent of the agreed contract price for up to three months after the works are complete. This is to ensure that the contractor is motivated to return and remedy any defects in the works. You will also need to consider how you are going to pay the contractor – monthly or upon certain milestones? For example, you may want to pay him ten per cent when he completes the foundations and another ten per cent once the structure is complete, etc. The

contract also requires the contractor to take out and maintain both a contractor's risks insurance policy and a public liability policy. It is advisable that you check the validity of the insurance policy.

The JCT have issued an updated form of this contract for when you employ a professional consultant in addition to the contractor. Because this is the contract that you are most likely to adopt it is reviewed clause by clause in Chapter 19 (see pages 162–164).

JCT Agreement for Minor Building Works 1998 (MW98) and JCT Intermediate Form of Building Contract 1998 (IFC98)

Where the works are more complex than merely "simple works", and an architect is employed independently of the contractor, the Minor Works Building agreement may be more suitable. Simple, short and low-value developments would be best suited to either the Agreement for Minor Building Works 1998 (MW98) or the Intermediate form of Building Contract 1998 (IFC98). MW98 is designed for simple contracts of six months' duration and a maximum value of £250,000. It is ideal where the works are priced on a fixed lump sum that is based on specifications, drawings or schedules, as opposed to bills of quantities.

If MW98 is unsuitable, consider IFC98. This contract is designed for projects with a value of £100,000–£400,000 and a contract period of less than 12 months, where there is no need for complex, specialist work. Both IFC98 and MW98 can be used outside the recommended limits of time and value.

JCT 1998 Standard Form With/Without/With Approximate Quantities (JCT98)

Where the works are not suited to either MW98 or IFC98, one of the JCT 1998 Standard Forms (JCT98) should be considered. These are heavyweight contracts that are divided into those with quantities, with approximate quantities and without quantities.

JCT98 is suitable for all types of building projects. However, the contractual provisions are intricate and wide-ranging. If it is proposed to use this form, you should seek professional advice. I suggest only using this contract where the value of the works exceed £500,000 and are complex in nature. If you are going to use this form of contract, you are likely to have employed a professional team consisting of an architect, engineer and quantity surveyor, who should also have formal appointments.

JCT Standard Form of Building Contract with Contractor's Design 1998 (WCD98)

This is another heavyweight design-and-build contract, where the contractor is responsible for both the design and build of the entire project.
I would only recommend this for the largest design-and-build jobs – in excess of £250,000. Design-and-build contracts are ideal for projects with simple design requirements, and their principal advantage is that the contractor is responsible for both the design and construction risks of the development. The contractual provisions are intricate and wide-ranging, and if it is proposed to use this form, I would urge you to seek professional advice.

Additional documents

You may want the contractor to procure a performance bond from its surety or bank. A performance bond is where a third party guarantees the performance of the contractor's obligations under the contract. A performance bond will typically be for ten per cent of the contract sum. You (or the contractor) may have to pay a premium for this. You could also make any payments to the contractor conditional upon providing the bond.

Collateral warranties

Until a few years ago, one of the cornerstones of contract law was a concept of privity of contract. This meant that only the parties to the contract could bring an action for a breach of it. Therefore, if a bank was lending money for a development, it would not be a party to the building contract, which would be between the employer and the contractor.

This means that if the employer went bust the bank would not be able to step in to complete the development in order to realise its security. Nor could it sue the contractor for any breaches of contract. To get round this problem lawyers would prepare a separate agreement between the contractor and the bank, where the contractor would guarantee its performance under the building contract to the bank. Now the bank has a direct contractual relationship with the contractor.

These agreements (known in the trade as collateral warranties) sometimes contain step-in rights, which entitle the bank to *(text continues on page 76)*

71

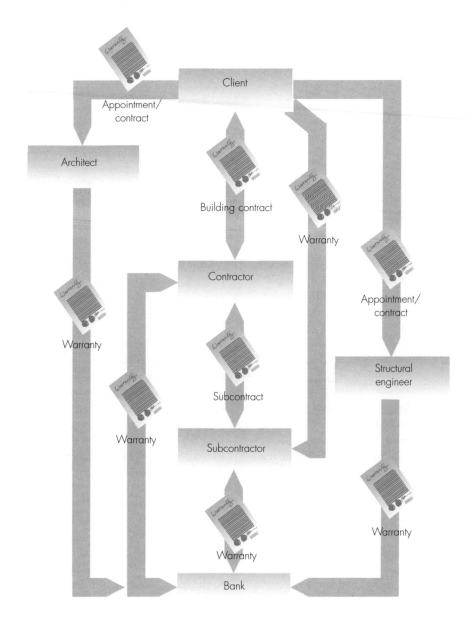

Client

Appointment/
contract

Architect

Building contract

Warranty

Contractor

Warranty

Appointment/
contract

Warranty

Structural
engineer

Subcontract

Warranty

Subcontractor

Warranty

Warranty

Warranty

Bank

Warranties
The goal of having collateral warranties is so that a contractual relationship
is created for the benefit of each interested party. Warranties are required where the
Contracts (Rights of Third Parties) Act 1999 is excluded.

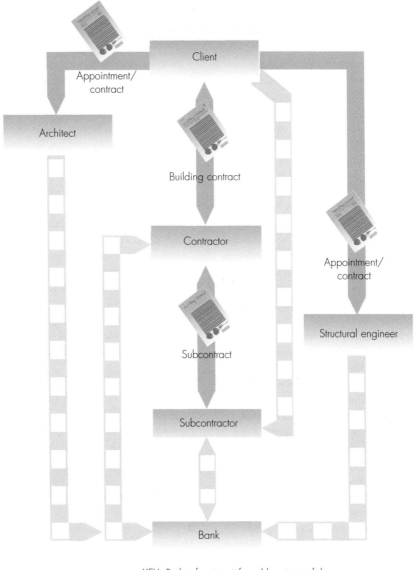

KEY: Right of action inferred by virtue of the Contract (Rights of Third Parties) Act 1999, so no physical warranty needs to be produced

Third Party Rights (no need for physical warranties)
Where the Contracts (Rights of Third Parties) Act 1999 has not been excluded from the contracts and the interested parties are named as having an interest in the respective contracts.

Food for thought

The way the construction industry currently operates is governed by contracts. The risks and responsibilities of each party are set out in the building contract and professional appointments. However, this is not the only way forward. Many construction projects have been very successful in the old-fashioned way, albeit dressed up with modern soundbites such as "partnering". Part of a legal advisor's job is to protect the client from risk and to allocate risk to the party that is best able to manage it. Typically, this will be the contractor, who is best placed to manage the majority of the risks that occur on the building site.

Not all risks can be covered, and this is what makes construction such a fascinating industry, and it is foolhardy to think that you can cover each and every risk. The number of external factors that are not the responsibility of either party are endless – from postal strikes and local authority strikes to weather that is not inclement but that any reasonable person would accept as being out of the ordinary.

Unfortunately, time is money, and with margins being cut ever tighter contractors will tender on the thinnest of margins, allowing no room for error and little float in the programmes; many then rely on the letter of the contract.

There is another way, which is fortunately gaining some momentum: forms of contract that are based on a non-adversarial approach. Rather than merely allocating risks, these contracts do so in a manner that establishes common ground and promotes harmony in the team. Unfortunately, none of these contracts are, in my opinion, suitable for self-builders and home improvers. However, all is not lost!

While you can still negotiate a formal contract, I strongly advise preparing a statement of principles which should focus the mind, encourage teamwork (as without a strong team no project is ever going to succeed) and foster a positive working environment – a partnership agreement.

An example of what a partnership statement between yourself and the contractor could provide for is shown below:

Statement of Principles between O'Neils Contractor and Moses Christie

O'Neils Contractors shall:

● Build the home at the plot adjoining 36 Newfields Street using the reasonable skill care and diligence in the design and construction of the development expected of a reasonably skilled design and build contractor experienced in projects of a similar size and complexity.

● Complete the project on or before 26 July 2005 and shall keep Moses and all other professionals regularly informed on progress.

Moses Christie shall:

● Pay O'Neils Contractors on time and in accordance with the architects certificates.

● Provide drawings and assistance to O'Neils in a timely fashion so as not to delay progress of the works.

Both Parties shall:

● Acknowlege that the building process has a certain element of uncertainty and will present problems that will need to be tackled as a partnership.

● Use their best endeavours to discuss potential problems before they arise.

● Work together as partners to achieve a solution that presents a "win-win" solution to the problem. In doing so O'Neils acknowledge that this may affect their profit margin and Moses accepts that this may delay the completion date for the development.

You could take this further and allocate various risks, in plain english, among the team. Other possible approaches are open book accounting, agreeing upon mediation as a forum for dispute resolution (rather than litigation), and accepting that "relief events" will impact on the entire team and not only the contractor.

These partnership agreements have little standing in law and are not things that can readily be sued upon (note the contradiction!), and to force a party into mediation goes against the grain of what mediation is all about – a voluntary, non-adversarial form of dispute resolution.

Having said all of the above, I do advise some form of partnership agreement or statement of principles. It will assist in setting the tone of the development and focus the minds of the parties, and is more likely to be referred to at meetings.

step into the shoes of its borrower (the developer) and allow the bank to complete the project. Strangely, many contractors resist step-in rights, even though they are in their favour, as without them they are faced with a half-finished project with no prospect of getting paid.

The British Property Federation (BPF) produces a standard form of collateral warranty. If you propose this form to your lending institution, you should be aware that they may request some amendments – for example, the BPF standard form contains a restriction that any copyright licence is subject to the contractors' or professionals' fees having been paid, as well as limiting its liability to the bank for any breach of the underlying building contract or professional appointment.

The Contract (Rights of Third Parties) Act 1999 now entitles, under certain circumstances, those parties who either expressly or by implication are intended to get a benefit from the contract to bring an action for its breach. Unfortunately, many larger banking institutions are a bit slow on the uptake and still prefer to keep their lawyers busy by producing reams of collateral warranties.

For most self-build projects it will be sufficient to procure NHBC Buildmark cover for the development. However, you will need to be aware that your lending institution may require collateral warranties in its favour from your professional team; if this is the case, I advise suggesting the virtues of the Contracts (Rights of Third Parties) Act to them.

KEY POINTS

- Do not rely upon an exchange of letters to appoint your professional team. Use a proper contract and ensure that at the very least it incorporates the provisions set out in this chapter and does not have any unacceptable limitations of liability.

- Select your building contract in accordance with the scope of your particular project. Your professionals should give you guidance as to which will be the most suitable form of contract.

- You do not need to be a party to a contract in order to bring an action under it, as long as the contract confers some benefit on you (as a third party) and does not expressly exclude the Contract (Rights of Third Parties) Act 1999.

- Consider having a partnership "agreement".

CHAPTER 7

Contract Law

Virtually every aspect of your project is going to be affected by contract law. Contracts are formed many times in the course of a normal day – buying a pint of milk or a bus ticket are all contracts that incorporate the same principles as buying a house or employing a contractor. This chapter examines the key elements of a contract, the terms (both express and implied) that make up the meat of the contract, and takes a look at what constitutes a breach of contract, the remedies available and compensation payable.

Contracts can be either written or oral. However, proving what was agreed with an oral contract is an uphill battle, so any agreements should always be made in writing.

Many houses are built and extensions completed with no written contract in place. Despite the obvious difficulties in trying to establish the responsibilities of the various parties, there are the obvious questions as to how much and when the contractor or supplier should be paid, and by when they should complete their works. The law provides that in such situations the employer must pay the contractor a reasonable fee for the work carried out and the contractor need only complete the works within a reasonable time. Clearly this acts in the contractor's favour as it removes the commercial reality of competition, and "reasonable" is an arbitrary term and could simply depend upon the mood of the judge on that particular day! Given this, it is infinitely more sensible to have a written contract.

Formation of contract

The three key elements for a valid contract are offer, acceptance and consideration. (Scottish law does not require consideration for a valid contract to be formed.) Without these three elements, you do not have a contract.

Offer

An offer to make a contract must be clear that it is an offer. The terms of the offer must be capable of being accepted. Tenders sent out to contractors are not offers, they are invitations to the contractors to make an offer. When the contractor comes back with a proposal based upon the terms in the tender documents, he is making you an offer, which you may or may not accept. Another example is when you go to an auction – when you make a bid, this is actually an offer which the auctioneer is at liberty to accept or reject. Once there is an offer to enter into a contract on definite legal terms, this offer can be accepted.

If you have made an offer to a contractor or supplier, it is possible that they will come back with a counteroffer (rather than accepting your initial offer). The ball is now in your court as to whether you want to accept this counteroffer, which destroys the previous offer you had made.

Acceptance

Acceptance of an offer can be inferred from the conduct of the other party, or it can be made expressly. For example, if you made an offer to the contractor on certain terms but never heard from him, yet he began to start work on site, his conduct is such that he is deemed to have accepted your offer. This is a simple scenario, as there tends to be a protracted period of negotiation in which it becomes almost impossible to ascertain who made an offer, on what terms and when this offer was accepted. You should be aware that mere silence cannot be construed as amounting to an acceptance of an offer.

The methods of acceptance of an offer raise interesting questions when the party making the offer wishes to revoke it. If you have a change of heart and wish to revoke an offer, you will need to communicate this intention before the offer is accepted, and the manner of communication must be such that the other party is aware of your intentions.

One of the most common forms of accepting an offer is by post. An offer is deemed to be accepted once a properly stamped and addressed letter is put in the postbox.

An offer can also be made subject to a time frame within which an acceptance must be made. If you do not state a time frame for acceptance and if a reasonable amount of time has lapsed, the offer can be deemed to have been revoked.

As you are aware, the sale and purchase of property can be conditional upon certain obligations being fulfilled (such as planning consent being obtained for the premises). If such a contract is made and the obligation is not fulfilled, the offer is no longer capable of being accepted.

Consideration

Consideration is a peculiarity of English law. In its most simple form it means that some benefit must be gained from the contract. This benefit is usually monetary – the cost of paying for a new car. But the anomaly is that it need not be of any commercial value, so paying £1 for a Jaguar is sufficient consideration. The courts have been known to construe some form of consideration (benefit) even when there is none on the face of the contract.

Capacity to make a contract

Generally, certain people cannot, in the eyes of the law, create a contractual relationship – minors, undischarged bankrupts and mentally "incapable" people.

Certainty

The terms of the offer must be sufficiently clear and precise to be capable of being accepted. Remember that any variation of the terms of the offer is a counteroffer. For example, an agreement to agree may invalidate the entire contract – or in the very least invalidate the clause to which it relates. An agreement to agree would be something along the lines of "A and B shall agree upon the price to be paid for the supply of the materials once they are supplied". Such a clause is both pointless and likely to be void for its uncertainty.

Duress and undue influence

Contracts that are entered into under duress or undue influence are void, as a contract is an agreement between two parties of their own free will. A contract

Case Study

Gus contracted with Usk Contractors to build an extension to his home. It transpired that Usk Contractors were having difficulty with their cash flow and bankruptcy seemed imminent, but more importantly it did not seem as though they would complete the works on time if they got into financial difficulties. This issue was critical, as Gus's wife had planned a birthday party for their three-year-old son in the new conservatory. Gus told Usk Contractors that if the works were completed on time he would make an additional payment to them. There was no written contract. Usk finished the work but were not paid the additional monies that were promised. In his defence Gus said that he was not prepared to pay Usk Contractors any more than that which Usk was contractually obliged to do. Gus's defence failed, as the benefit of completing the works on time was considered additional consideration and the new promise was binding.

If, on the other hand, Usk Contractors tried to pull a fast one on Gus and he offered the additional payments to them under duress or pretence of fraud, he would be entitled not to make the additional payments to Usk.

can also be void if it is an unconscionable bargain; however, what constitutes an unconscionable bargain is a hard test – it is unlikely that naivety, ignorance or weak-mindedness would be sufficient defences.

Letters of intent

Letters of intent are commonly used in the construction industry when the parties are close to agreeing the terms of the contract but there is an urgency to commence the works. Letters of intent are merely a letter from the employer to the contractor expressing the employer's intention to enter into the contract. The letter will allow the contractor to commence with the ordering of materials, or even to commence works on site. The employer will reimburse the contractor an agreed amount which must be stated in the letter of intent.

Terms of a contract

The terms of a contract can either be express or implied. Express terms are those that are agreed by the parties and written into the contract. Implied terms are those terms that the contract may be subject to, depending upon the custom of a particular industry, legislation or the courts.

The terms of a contract are generally going to be the small print at the back of a contract. I strongly suggest that you take time out to read the small print to know what obligations are expected of you pursuant to the contract. Some of these terms may not be valid by virtue of the unfair terms in consumer contracts regulations, which are discussed later in this chapter.

Express terms

These are the easiest terms of the contract to identify. They are written into a contract and express what the parties have agreed. There is a general rule of law that once the terms of the contract have been agreed, one cannot use external evidence to show that the other party has misinterpreted a statement in the contract. In practical terms, this means that the correspondence relating to negotiations may be excluded in trying to understand the terms of the contract.

When reading contracts, it is common to find contractors and suppliers limiting their liability for defective services and workmanship. Some even go as far as wanting the employer to indemnify them for any costs incurred as a consequence of unsuccessful legal actions brought against them. With respect to clauses that limit liability, you need to take a commercial decision as to whether the limitation of liability is sufficient to cover your potential losses against the cost of the works and the availability of other suitable contractors.

Implied terms

Terms may be implied into the contract, depending upon the customs of an industry, or by legislation (such as the Supply of Goods and Services Act) or by the courts. Certain industries have their own way of dealing with disputes or arranging deliveries, and these terms may be implied into the contract. The Sale of Goods and Supply of Services Acts imply

Case Study

Darren wanted to build a new house and intended to contract with Alexis Contractors to build the home. The intention was to enter into a design-and-build contract, and Darren would undertake a project-management role. There were some issues in relation to the negotiation of the contract that were taking some time, the principle one being that Darren wanted Alexis Contractors to take the responsibility for any unforeseen ground conditions. Darren did not feel that this should be his responsibility, as the contractors had sufficient time to carry out a site investigation.

Time pressed on and a sense of urgency was creeping in. Alexis had by far the best bid and the best reputation, so Darren decided to write a letter of intent to Alexis, entitling them to order materials up to the cost of £20,000.

In the meantime correspondence and draft contracts were still going backwards and forwards in order to ascertain which party was going to take responsibility for the ground conditions of the site. Darren would write to Alexis Contractors stating that it was a condition of the contract that the responsibility for the ground certain terms in a contract – for example, in a contract for the supply of services it is implied that the services will be carried out with reasonable skill and care and using suitable materials. Finally, the courts may imply terms in order to make the contract effective.

Unfair contract terms

Contractors and suppliers do not have an entirely free hand as to the terms provided for in their contracts. English law provides some protection to consumers in the Unfair Contract Terms Act 1977 and the Unfair Terms in Consumer Contracts Regulations 1999.

Section 3 of the Unfair Contract Terms Act (UCTA) deals with situations where one enters into contracts as a consumer or on the standard terms of business of another business. Many of the contracts that you, as a consumer, are likely to enter into with suppliers and contractors will be on their standard terms – as opposed to negotiating a bespoke contract each time you need some timber! The law is unclear whether the standard forms of construction contract – the JCT forms of contract – would be considered "standard" for the purposes of the Act.

Under UCTA there are certain exclusions in contracts that are void, for example:

● You can never exclude or restrict liability for negligence causing personal injury or death. This is news to many fairground operators and contractors who habitually try to exclude such liability. Such a clause is void in the eyes of the law.

conditions would be theirs, then Alexis Contractors would reply by refuting this and passing the obligation onto Darren.

Eventually works got underway on site without this issue being resolved. Unfortunately, there were serious problems with the ground conditions, and substantial work was required to make the ground suitable for the foundations of the house. Alexis Contractors put in a claim for loss and expense and an extension of time. With whom did the responsibility for the ground conditions rest?

The principle in law is that there is a contract as soon as the last form is sent out and received without an objection being taken to it. Clearly the difficulty is deciding which party fired the last shot. In this case Darren had sent out his form of contract, and while this contract was with Alexis Contractors they moved in on site and began the construction works, and even accepted and cashed an interim payment. Only then did they write back to Darren, stating that they were not prepared to accept the terms of his contract and insisting on their form. The risk rests with the contractors.

● If you enter into a hire purchase scheme for a JCB or other item, you are entitled to rely upon the fact that the "seller" has sufficient ownership of that item in order to enter into a hire purchase scheme with you. The seller cannot exclude or restrict these basic assumptions of ownership.

● In hire purchase agreements the seller cannot exclude or restrict liability as to the fitness for the purpose for which those items are supplied, nor can the seller exclude or restrict their quality.

The act also provides a catch-all provision where some clauses that are both unreasonable and restrict the scope of performance under the contract are void. The test of reasonableness is abstract and depends upon the social and commercial norms at the time, the status of the parties that have entered into the contract, and the nature of the contract itself. The courts will look to what the parties contemplated at the time of entering into the contract, the respective negotiating strengths of the parties, and whether the goods were bespoke.

Unfair terms in consumer contracts

One of the advantages of the European Union is the introduction of legislation that puts some power back into the hands of the consumer. One such example is the Unfair Terms in Consumer Contracts Regulations 1999. These regulations are relevant to home builders and improvers, as they relate specifically to consumer contracts. In order to be a consumer in the eyes of the law, you must conduct your transactions outside the scope of the ordinary course of a business. These regulations will not apply if the terms of the contract have been individually negotiated; clearly, certain items are always going to be negotiated, such as the price of the services. Accordingly, you will be looking at the instances when you buy goods from the builder's warehouse and there are reams of small print attached to your invoice.

The regulations work in a very simple manner. If a contract contains a clause that is regarded as being unfair, that clause is deemed to be void and is struck out, but the remainder of the contract continues to be effective.

What kind of term is regarded as being unfair under the act? This is the million pound question. An unfair term is "any term which, contrary to the requirements of good faith, causes a significant imbalance in the parties' rights and obligations arising under the contract to the detriment of the consumer".

In deciding what falls into this definition of unfairness, the act guides the judges to consider:

● The bargaining strengths of the parties.

● Whether the consumer had an inducement to enter into the contract.

● Whether the seller acted fairly and equitably to the purchaser.

If a supplier puts an unfair term in small print into a contract in an effort to conceal it from the consumer, the regulations will act against the supplier. The courts are likely to conclude that such actions will lend weight to the arguments by the consumer that such a clause is unfair.

If a clause is drafted so that the consumer cannot understand it, again the courts are more likely to regard this clause as being unfair and the clause will be struck out.

Performance

Clearly the obligations of each party to the contract must be completed in full. Sometimes events outside of the control of each party have the effect of making the performance of the contract impossible. You will see such terms referred to as forces majeure (acts of god). Building contracts sometime try to shift the risk of unforeseen conditions onto the contractor – examples are the risks associated with unforeseen ground conditions, inclement weather, and even shortage in labour and materials as a result of strikes.

If the contractor fails to complete the works as agreed in the contract, the employer need not pay. If a contractor installed heating in a house but the heating did not work properly, the employer need not pay him anything and the contractor could not recover for the works done. Clearly the courts tend to construe exceptions to this principle, as the employer is getting some benefit from the partially completed works. If there is a substantial performance payment should be made, but the employer will make a claim for the omissions or defects in the works.

Case Study

Frankie bought some timber from a timber merchant. The timber already had screws drilled into it, so that when Frankie came to install the timber he would not need to drill the screws into the timber – it was "ready-made'.

When he purchased the timber he was asked to sign a contract that excluded all the timber merchant"s liability for damage. However, the timber merchant told him that the exclusion related only to the suitability of the screws, and not the quality of the timber itself.

When Frankie got home and began to install the timber he noticed that the timber was both warped and split. In this circumstance the timber merchant could not exclude his liability for the defective timber, despite the principle that written terms (the sale contract) supersede oral terms (what Frankie was told by the salesperson). The reason is because such a limitation of liability clause is constructed against the party that is relying on it.

In this instance the timber merchants are unlikely to have drawn Frankie's attention sufficiently to the limitation of liability clause in the contract; especially as the salesman focused Frankie's mind on excluding its liability for the suitability of the screws only.

Another scenario is where you, as the employer, know that the contractor or supplier does not intend to perform his future obligations. Rather than wait for the non-performance, what can you do about it? As the employer, you can repudiate the contract, either expressly or implicitly by your actions.

Case Study

Daniel and Carla wanted to buy a house and had entered into a contract with Zepheria to purchase his house. Unfortunately, Zepheria intended to sell his house to John and Jane. Zepheria's intention to sell to John and Jane must be clear and beyond reasonable doubt. Clearly in this scenario Zepheria has repudiated the contract with Daniel and Carla. Here, the innocent parties have a right of action against Zepheria. Daniel and Carla can either wait for the breach to occur (when Zepheria sells to John and Jane) or sue immediately for a breach.

Rights of third parties

One of the fundamental principles of English law was that only the parties to a contract could bring an action for a breach under that contract. For example, if a husband entered into a contract and was unable to sue the contractor, the wife could not step into his shoes and sue the contractor, as the contractor did not enter into a contract with her.

This principle was turned on its head

in 1999, and now, by virtue of the Contracts (Rights of Third Parties) Act 1999, a third party – being one that was not a party named in the contract – may enforce the terms of the contract if the contract expressly provides that he may, or (subject to a few conditions) the term purports that a benefit is conferred on the third party.

Unfortunately, many contractors and suppliers exclude this act from their agreements as they want to limit the number of people that can sue them. If this act is excluded the contract will typically say something like "the provisions of the Contracts (Rights of Third Parties) Act 1999 are excluded from this agreement".

If you think that a third party may want to sue under the contract, I suggest stating in the contract that "X" has the benefit of the terms of the agreement pursuant to the Contracts (Rights of Third Parties) Act 1999.

Remedies for breach of contract

If there has been a breach of contract, there are two main options available to the aggrieved party – damages for the breach of contract and specific performance.

If you are going to bring an action for a breach of contract, you must have suffered some loss. Consider who you are going to sue, and consider whether they have sufficient assets. There is little point in suing a company that is genuinely insolvent, or an individual who is bankrupt.

If you are going for damages, you must be aware of the overriding principle that the damages you are entitled to are those damages that would put you in the position that you would be in had the contract been properly performed.

In many consumer contracts you will see a cap on liability, and it is very important that if you do decide to accept such a term in the contract, the cap is sufficient to cover your losses – the level of the cap could be balanced against something like the cost of rebuilding your house. The cap could also be unenforceable by virtue of UCTA.

I suggest capping the damages that a contractor or supplier is entitled to for any breach that you may commit. You can do this by inserting a provision whereby the contractor or supplier shall not be entitled to loss of profits or

Case Study

Schwim were contracted to build Mr Thorpe a swimming pool in his garden. Mr Thorpe was a big man and specifically wanted a pool that was 2.4m deep. On completion the pool was found to be 2.1m deep. Mr Thorpe was outraged. However, there was no adverse affect on the value of the house or on the enjoyment of the diving, but there was clearly a breach. Here, the courts are likely to award only nominal damages for the breach, rather than the cost of reinstatement. (The facts of this case might be different if a party had a watch destroyed whilst being repaired, as the cost of its replacement would be the true value of the loss.)

consequential losses arising from any breach of contract of the employer (or his agents or employees).

The damages that are recoverable are those that are in the reasonable

Case Study

Isaac had decided that he was going to carry out the bulk of the physical work for his new house, and he subcontracted each of the specialist elements. Isaac had a tight programme, as he wanted to get the roof on before the winter; more importantly, he had contracted to sell his existing home on 1 October. At the later stages there were two specialist subcontractors employed on the project: subcontractor X was to deliver and erect the pre-fabricated frame, and subcontractor Y was going to clad the building in brick. Subcontractor X could not perform his bargain. Irrespective of Isaac's claim against X, he had an obligation to mitigate his losses, which at this stage looked severe. He had contracted to sell his home, the cladding contractor (subcontractor Y) was incurring losses, and there was the untold damage of the onset of winter with the prospect of no roof.

It was not acceptable for Isaac to sit back and watch his claim mount up. He had to make reasonable steps to mitigate his losses and to employ another subcontractor to complete the prefabricated frame.

Case Study

Harry Contractors had failed to use reasonable skill and care in constructing Sally's house. Sally was an IT whiz and had instructed Harry Contractors to build a special office so that she could store all her computer data and equipment there. Sally failed to use a proper building contract, but there was an exchange of letters instructing Harry Contractors to do the works for an agreed fee.

This Harry Contractors did. Fortunately for Sally, it is implied in all contracts for the supply of services that the contractor will use reasonable skill and care in carrying out the works and will use suitable materials.

Harry Contractors failed to do this, and the roof of the new office began to leak that winter. The water destroyed the computers, disks and all her data; not only that, but the floor

contemplation of the contracting parties at the time of entering into the contract. So if there is some form of special loss suffered by the aggrieved party that the party in breach is not aware of, nor could reasonably be aware of, the aggrieved party cannot claim for these monies.

In most cases you will be able to recover monies for the breach and the cost of remediating the breach. You will not be able to recover damages where the loss is considered too remote.

If there is a breach and you suffer a loss, you cannot simply sit back and watch your losses mount. There is a duty on the aggrieved party to minimise (mitigate) his losses.

Specific performance

The courts do not use this remedy much. The principle of specific performance is

where the courts compel the party in breach to complete their part of the bargain. It is unlikely that you will want the contractor back onto your site after the breach, so this remedy can be academic. The courts employ this remedy in contracts for the sale and purchase of homes. Here, the courts are much more likely to order the seller to sell his home to the buyer (or conversely, the buyer to buy the home).

Specific performance is regarded as a discretionary remedy, and it is up to the courts whether or not to apply it – you can request it when you make your claim, but you may not necessarily get it.

There are time limits when you bring a claim. For most contracts this is six years from the date of the breach (in construction contracts, this is sometimes stated as being from the date of practical was flooded, destroying the carpets. Sally's cat – Lucifer, a rare Persian that she kept for breeding (and as a pet) – drowned.

Sally made a claim for the lost computer equipment and loss of profits from her breeding cat. The claim for the computer equipment was successful – Harry Contractors were aware what Sally intended to use the office for and what she intended to store in it; however, Harry Contractors did argue that Sally failed to mitigate her losses by failing to back up her data at a separate remote location. The loss of breeding profits from Lucifer was considered too remote and not in the contemplation of the parties at the time that the contract was entered into.

completion of the contract). Some contracts that are signed as deeds have a 12-year limitation period within which to bring an action.

Practical considerations

This chapter has examined the law that governs how contracts are made and governed. But there are practical considerations that you need to be sure of in relation to preparing and entering into contracts.

When you get a contract, go through the following steps:

● Take the time to thoroughly read the contract and ensure that you understand it. If there are terms that you do not understand – ask.

● Decide which parties are going to enter into the contract. It may be advisable to carry out a company search against the contracting company. Companies House can do this for you for a small fee.

● Highlight any clauses that you are not happy with. You could either strike them out or make manuscript amendments. Both parties must initial any amendments.

● When it comes to signing the contract, make sure that the company correctly executes it by a director and a second director or the company secretary; a company seal may also be used. If a partnership is signing the agreement, ensure that each partner signs the contract and that their signatures are validly witnessed.

KEY POINTS

● Contracts are formed in every aspect of life. Think how many contracts you enter into in a day.

● Written contracts are critical to evidence what was agreed. Do not rely on oral contracts.

● In order to have a valid contract, you must have an offer whose terms are sufficiently clear and precise to be capable of acceptance.

● There must be an acceptance of the offer and some form of benefit flowing from the agreement.

● Terms in the contract are best expressed in writing, but they can be implied by legislation.

● Make sure unfair terms are excluded from consumer contracts.

● Third parties that are not the original contracting parties can bring an action for breach if the contract conferred a benefit on them.

● If there is a breach of contract, you are entitled to the damages that would put you in the position that you would be in had the contract been properly performed.

● You have a responsibility to mitigate any damages that you may suffer as a consequence of another party's breach of contract.

CHAPTER 8

Clauses Specific to Building Contracts

At its core a construction contract will be for the construction of a home to a set cost, desired quality and stipulated time frame. Unfortunately, the reality of the construction process rarely follows the pre-determined path that you have planned. To deal with this, construction contracts have clauses to allow for a certain amount of flexibility.

Construction contracts allow the employer to:

● Issue variations to the scope of the agreed project.

● Grant an extension of time to the contractor to complete the project beyond the agreed completion date.

● Entitle the employer to a daily rate of damages payable by the contractor for each day that the contractor is late in completing the works.

Each of these provisions and others that are peculiar to supply and construction contracts used in the building industry are examined in this chapter.

Variations

When you approach a builder or an architect, it pays to have a firm idea of what you want to achieve. Once they are instructed to start the project there is the scope to change your mind, but such changes may cost you dearly, as materials would have been ordered, programmes planned and drawings completed.

Most building contracts have a provision to allow the employer to change (within reason) the scope of the works. You may need to vary the contract because you have changed your mind, or because as the work proceeds difficulties transpire that make the original plans ineffective.

When the contractor makes his bid he agrees to carry out those works for a set fee, so if the contractor makes a claim for additional money because the works were more expensive than he had originally anticipated, this is not something he can claim for. It is a reflection of his inability to correctly price for the works.

A detailed brief with detailed drawings limits any potential arguments put forward by a contractor for additional money, on the basis that he is not being asked to do something greater than that which he was originally instructed.

Most building contracts provide for the architect to issue an instruction to the contractor. It is this instruction which states the extent of the variation to the works.

The JCT contracts allow the architect to:

● Alter or modify the design, quality or quantity of the works as shown on the contract drawings or contract bills.

● Make any addition, omission or substitution of any work.

● Alter the kind or standard of any materials being used on the works.

● Remove from the site any works and materials.

The contract must provide for the architect to have the power to issue any variations, otherwise he will be liable to you, as the employer, for the cost of any such variations.

Omissions from the works will be priced according to the bills of quantity. Variations that are additional to the existing works but use similar materials would also be priced with reference to the bills. If the variation is not one that can be priced in accordance with the bills, the additional works should be priced in accordance with a fair valuation of those works.

All variations entitle the contractor for additional time to complete the works, and may also entitle him to loss and expense. Finally, it would be unwise not to issue a variation to the contract where it is obvious that one is required in order for the works to continue, such as unforeseen difficulties in the ground conditions.

If you did not issue a variation notice where one is required, the contractor can either carry out these works (and you, as the employer, would be obliged to pay him), or he could sue you for a breach of contract.

Extensions of time

A delay to the planned completion date is likely to happen to the best planned building ventures; it is an unfortunate fact that this is a regular occurrence in many construction projects. The key in managing delays is to establish their cause. The works may not finish on time because you have issued a variation to

the scope of the works; alternatively, the cause may be down to some failure on the part of the contractor or supplier.

Despite the frustration that a delay in the completion of the project may have, it may, under certain circumstances, be preferable to accept this fact of life and amend the construction timetable as best you can. Alternatively, if the cause of the delay is not caused by you, you may wish to pursue this matter with the contractor or the supplier, particularly if they have caused delays to other trades or have affected your projected cash flow.

Delays tend to have a knock-on, or domino, effect on trade, particularly where there is a tight programme. Most prudent house builders build a float to account for unforeseen eventualities into their programme of works. However, despite this float, certain tasks will be on the critical path. Delays to the tasks on the critical path can have a profound impact on the project's timetable for completion.

There are three general types of delay that can affect any construction job:

● Delays caused by you (the employer).

● Delays caused by the contractor or supplier.

● Delays caused by circumstances outside both parties' control.

This section looks at the general approach taken by standard building contracts in relation to delays caused by these three circumstances, and also looks at the approach to take in the event that there is no contract in place. Your individual contract may deal with delays differently.

Effect of a delay

If the contractor is at fault for the delays – for example, if he failed to order sufficient materials or did not employ enough manpower to complete the job, there is no reason why you should be at a loss. Many building contracts (including the JCT range) have a liquidated damages provision in the contract. Liquidated damages are a daily rate of damages that you are entitled to from the contractor for any delays to the proposed date for practical completion where the contractor is at fault. A liquidated damages clause does not prevent you from bringing an action in the courts for a breach of contract.

If you (or your agents) caused the delay, you will have to grant the contractor an extension of time to complete the project, and the contract may also entitle the contractor to loss and expense. The amount of time granted to the contractor to complete the project must be a reasonable amount of time, having regard to the circumstances of the delay or variation. The effect of granting an extension of time extends the date for practical completion and delays the date on which liquidated damages become due.

General contract terms

There are a few industry norms when it comes to establishing which delays are the cause of the employer and which are the responsibility of the contractor. These are discussed below, and are likely to be expressed in the contract.

Employer's risk

The following circumstances are examples of where you (or your agent) may have to grant the contractor an extension of time (employer's risk). They are normally referred to as "relevant events" in the building contract:

● Force majeure (act of God). This covers extreme events such as floods, earthquakes and war.

● Exceptionally adverse weather conditions. The key here is "exceptionally". The contractor must plan his works according to the seasons that he is likely to encounter. For example, a fit-out should take place in winter, once the roof is on. An example of what would constitute exceptionally adverse weather would be snow or frost in the summer months.

● Civil commotion, strikes affecting the trade employed on the works or engaged in the preparation, manufacture or transportation of goods for the works.

● A failure by you, the employer, or one of your agents (such as the architect), in providing goods, materials, plans etc. that you had agreed to provide to the contractor.

● A failure of a local authority to carry out certain works – for example, with plots of land the authorities may have a responsibility to lay pipes etc.

● A failure by you, the employer, or your agents to give the contractor access to the site.

Should you be at fault in causing the contractor delay, it does not automatically follow that he is entitled to additional money as well as additional time.

A contractor's claim for loss and expense is a complex area. However, as a simple guide, the contractor may be entitled to more money if his costs have increased because his plant or labour have become more "inefficient" because of the delay, or if he can prove that he would have lost profits had it not been for the delay. As with all such claims, the contractor must show that his losses were a direct consequence of the delaying event.

Contractor's risk

Circumstances where the contractor is not usually entitled to an extension of time (contractor's risk) are where the delays to the works are caused by:

● A shortage of goods and materials.

● A shortage of labour.

● The opening up and examination of work that is found not to be in accordance with the contract.

● Inclement weather – it is only exceptionally adverse weather that would normally entitle the contractor to more time, not merely bad weather.

Minimising the cause of the delay

Both parties have a duty to minimise the effect of the delay upon the project's completion. Even the contractor has a duty to minimise the impact of the employer's risks for delay (such as exceptionally adverse weather). However, the contractor's duty does not normally involve extending his work outside his normal working hours (unless of course the contractor caused the delay).

Where there is no contract

It is not uncommon to find construction works ongoing without a contract in place. A delay in completion is a perfect example of the advantages of having a written contract agreed and signed between you and the contractor/supplier. Where there is no written contract, the contractor need only complete his works within a reasonable time. What would be considered as being a reasonable amount of time depends upon (in part) how much control the contractor had in relation to the events causing the delay.

Do you see the advantage in having a written contract? What is or is not a reasonable time is very difficult to quantify and will generate greater uncertainty for the date upon which you would expect to have your home completed. The other disadvantage in not having a written contract is that you would have to sue the contractor for damages, rather than being entitled to an agreed and pre-determined daily rate of damages (liquidated damages) for each day that the contractor is late.

If a claim for an extension of time is made you should check to ensure that the contractor has made his claim within the time frame required by the contract. If the claim is made outside this time frame, his claim may be void.

Claims for loss and expense

As we have seen, under certain circumstances the contractor can claim for additional time within which to complete the project.

As with extensions of time, there are contractual norms that identify circumstances where the contractor is entitled to loss and expense. The potential claims for loss and expense that are considered in this section are those that arise directly out of the provisions of the contract. Either party has the scope to make a monetary claim for a breach of the contract itself. Under most JCT contracts the type of incidences that a contractor can claim additional money for are:

● Late receipt of information – for example permissions, drawings and other pieces of information that the contractor needs in order to do his job.

● Where the employer instructs that works are opened up and it is found that the works are in accordance with the contract. Most JCT forms have a provision where the employer can open up the works to check whether the works have been completed in accordance with the contract. If the employer has wrongly assumed that the works are not in accordance with the contract, the contractor can make a claim for loss and expense.

● Delays in the employer carrying out works or a delay to procure materials that he has agreed to procure.

● A failure of the employer to give the contractor suitable access to the site.

As with any monetary claim, the contractor will need to show some real loss. It is not sufficient to show cause but no loss.

For most disputes where there is a breach of contract, the measure of damages available is twofold: those that flow naturally from the breach, and those which the parties would reasonably have contemplated at the time of entering into the contract.

A claim for loss and expense within the framework of most construction contracts generally only provides for direct loss and expense (check the wording of your individual contract). The word "direct" is the important factor, as it means that the contractor can only claim for losses arising directly out of the failure of the employer to perform under the contract. As with all civil law claims, the contractor will need to show that the direct losses incurred were, on the balance of probabilities, a direct consequence of the act/omission of the employer (pursuant to those acts/omissions which give rise to a potential claim and are listed in the building contract).

As with claims for extensions of time, there are strict time limits laid down in the contract within which any claim for loss and expense must be brought. One of the first things to check is whether the contractor is not out of time in making his claim.

It will usually be for your architect to assess the validity of any claim for loss and expense. The amount that is due is decided by the quantity surveyor. The types of things that a contractor will claim for are:

● Increase in his overheads and running costs.

● Loss of profit that he would have been able to make elsewhere.

● Interest.

Damages for delayed completion (liquidated damages)

Liquidated damages is the trade term given to a sum of money that is payable to the employer (you) by the contractor in the event that the contractor does not complete his work by the completion date specified in the building contract. A delay in completion by the contractor may cause you financial loss – for example, you may have agreed with your mortgage lender that your repayments shall only commence on the date that your house is expected to be practically complete; if this date is delayed, you may be repaying your mortgage with no house to live in.

The advantages of having a liquidated damages clause are that the damages are both fixed in advance of any breach of contract and can be recovered without proof of loss. Therefore, a liquidated damages clause gives you certainty of how much money you are entitled to, and it avoids the time and expense involved in proving a claim for damages caused by the contractor's delay.

The contract must clarify the start and end dates for the contractor's work. Without a proposed date for practical completion, you will be unable to establish the trigger date from which the liquidated damages must run.

Liquidated damages will usually be expressed in the appendix of the contract as a financial amount, which should be expressed as a daily rate. This means that

the contractor must pay you this sum for each day that the works are delayed beyond the agreed completion date.

You should avoid having a liquidated damages clause that expresses the figure payable as either a weekly or monthly rate, or as a percentage of the contract sum. If you do this, you may invalidate your right to claim liquidated damages because the proposed figure may be perceived to be a "penalty" and not a genuine pre-estimate of your losses.

There are a lot of cases that discuss what amount the courts would regard as being a penalty. A good rule is that any sum that would be regarded as being "extravagant and unconscionable" would be regarded as a penalty. Contrast this with the greatest loss that you could possibly have proved as a result of the contractor's breach of contract.

You may still get your liquidated damages if you are unable to estimate your losses, and even if the amount is regarded as too high it is not unknown for the courts to reduce the level of liquidated damages (rather than to entirely invalidate the contractual provision).

It is not uncommon for the contractor to try to cap the figure for liquidated damages to either the value of the contract sum or a percentage of it. If there is such a cap, it would be worth considering incorporating a right for you to terminate the contract in the event that the cap is reached; otherwise, you may be incurring losses that you cannot recover.

The entire premise of liquidated damages is the rate the contractor is to pay you for each day that he is late in achieving practical completion. If the contractor is late because he has been delayed by you or one of your agents (ie a last-minute change in the design), unless you have given the contractor a suitable extension of time to complete his works, the liquidated damages provision may be invalid.

Where you have awarded the contractor an extension of time to complete the works, the date that triggers the payment of the liquidated damages is the revised completion date. The circumstances that require you to grant an extension of time are usually set out in the contract. For example, delays caused by you will entitle the contractor to an extension of time, while delays caused by a shortage of materials, equipment or labour are not usually reasons that allow the contractor an extension of time to complete the works.

Completion

Practical completion (referred to in the trade as PC) is a very significant stage in any project. Not only does it mean that the works are signed off as being complete, but it also marks:

● The beginning of the defects liability period.

● The transfer of risk in the building's insurance back to its owner.

● The end of any liquidated damages liability.

● The release of part of the contractor's retention.

At the time of signing a building contract (again I shall refer to the JCT standard forms) you are likely to have agreed that you, as the employer, will retain about five per cent of the contractor's contract sum until the practical completion certificate is issued. This sum of money is called a retention and is supposed to represent the contractor's profit element on a job. Its aim is to motivate the contractor to do his work well (it is shame that a retention is even required).

Once your architect has inspected the works and is satisfied that (save for any minor snagging items) the works are substantially complete, he will issue a practical completion certificate to the contractor. At this time you may wish to release some of the retention (say 50 per cent). You will now retain two and a half per cent of the contract sum until the end of the defects liability period.

Some contracts allow for sectional completion of the works. This means that the architect can certify a certain section of the house as having attained PC while works are continuing in the remainder of the house. If you decide to incorporate a provision for partial possession, you need to ensure that you will not delay the contractor in carrying out the remainder of the works, thus giving rise to a claim for an extension of time. The period for the making good of defects of the part commences, as does the responsibility of insuring that part of the works on the issuing of the practical completion of that part.

If you are going to have NHBC Buildmark cover, you need to consider how this is going to be achieved at practical completion, particularly if it is your intention to sell the home upon practical completion. It is common sense for the house builder to ensure that the house will pass the certifying process before requesting the NHBC inspector to attend the site. In the case of the NHBC you need to give at least 24 hours notice for the final inspection. Once the NHBC (or similar) inspector is satisfied with the works, he will issue the Buildmark cover note to the house builder.

Defects liability period

The length of the defect liability period is specified in the building contract. I recommend that this should be 12 months from the date of practical completion. This is the period in which the contractor is obliged to return and remedy any defects in his works that become apparent. Defects are commonly defined as "defects, excessive shrinkage or other faults", so a contractor need not return to the property to repair minor shrinkage. Damage due to frost occurring before practical completion is the responsibility of the contractor; damage due to frost after practical completion is the responsibility of the employer.

Contractors can be reluctant to return to remedy defects during the defects liability period. In order to motivate them, half the retention is released upon practical completion, and the other half is retained until the end of the defects liability period. Another good motivating factor tends to be to show that it is in their interest to remedy the defect, as if they do not remedy the defect they are in breach of contract and you may instruct another contractor to do the works and recover the money from the errant contractor. The defects liability period is

an opportunity for contractors to ensure that their workmanship is not in breach of the standard of workmanship expressed (or implied) in the contract.

At the end of the defects liability period your architect will issue a making good of defects certificate and you should release the remainder of the retention.

Termination of the contract

Building contracts tend to have a provision where either the employer or the contractor may, under certain circumstances, terminate the contract. The grounds for termination for each party, and the mechanics of termination, are different in each case.

As a general guide to industry norms, the following are examples of the grounds upon which an employer may terminate the contract:

● Contractor suspends his works.

● Contractor neglects to remedy defective works.

● Contractor becomes insolvent (note: this is not a breach of contract).

● Contractor is guilty of taking bribes.

Examples of the grounds upon which a contractor can terminate the contract are:

● Employer fails to pay.

● Employer obstructs the contractor.

● Employer becomes insolvent.

Examples of the grounds upon which either the contractor or the employer can terminate the contract are:

● War.

● Damage due to an insured event.

Grounds for the suspension of works are:

● Acts of god.

● Civil commotion.

● An insured risk.

KEY POINTS

● A contractor may claim for an extension of time within which to complete the works. The grounds and procedure for making a claim for an extension of time would be set out in the contract.

● An extension of time delays the date that liquidated damages become due.

● If you do not have a written contract specifying an agreed completion date or time frame to complete the works, the contractor need only complete the works within a reasonable time.

● A claim for an extension of time does not necessarily entitle the contractor to additional money.

● A contractor may be able to make a claim for direct losses and expenses. The grounds and procedure for making such a claim would be set out in the contract.

● If your contract allows you to propose a figure for liquidated damages, propose a figure that represents a genuine (daily) pre-estimate of your losses. A figure that is too high may be regarded as a penalty and will invalidate the clause.

● If you propose to withold monies that are properly due to the contractor then you must issue a witholding notice (usually within 5 days of the contractor presenting his invoice). The notice must set out how much monies are being witheld and why.

● If the contractor has missed the agreed completion date because of an event for which he was entitled to be awarded an extension of time, you must award the contractor a reasonable extension of time to complete his works; you will then be able to claim your liquidated damages from the revised completion date.

● Read your contract – the topics discussed in this chapter are only the general norms, and each contract will have its own, unique provisions.

CHAPTER 9

Contract and Site Administration

Building contracts and professional appointments are unlike contracts for the sale and purchase of goods. They are a guide not only as to the standard and scope of the works to be carried out and the amount and frequency of payments, but also how to manage the works. Most building contracts lay down formal steps to take when making (or withholding) payments, issuing variations to the works and dealing with disputes. Managing a site and the trades on it is a complex task, which is not helped by the dangerous nature of construction. This chapter also looks at how to run a safe site and what regulations you must consider in relation to this aspect of construction.

You have probably decided upon your programme of works, but have you considered whether the access and services of the site are adequate for the trades? Are there restrictions on noise levels and the time that works can be carried out? How does this affect your programme of works? These are all questions that should be thought through before works commence, and arguably, even before the contract is placed.

Site meetings

Having regular site meetings is obvious, but unfortunately they are rarely carried out. Depending upon the nature of your project, I suggest having a formal meeting once a week with the entire team. Meetings need not be long – about 30 minutes should do it. The aim of these meetings would be to iron out existing or potential problems and to assist each profession to communicate with each other. The building industry is incredibly fragmented, and it does not occur naturally for architects and contractors to work in harmony, as it is their nature to think differently; however, both parties must be reminded of the shared goal – the completion of an amazing building that both can be proud of.

Plan for each of your site meetings with a formal notice requesting attendance, an agenda and minutes formalising what was said at the last meeting. The parties should then agree these minutes. Such management not only helps the progress of the works, but also assists in adducing evidence in the event of a dispute.

You will also be faced with minor annoyances, and again it pays to focus on the ultimate goal – the completion of your building on time, to budget and to the required specification. Diverting your attention on pointless finger-pointing exercises and "what ifs" only diverts energy from this goal. This is where your skills as the employer and project manager come into play; it is not an easy job, and you must be at your pragmatic and diplomatic best.

Site inspections

Most formal appointments of an architect will require them to attend the site at appropriate intervals to ensure that the works are being carried out in accordance with the designs, employer's requirements and building contract. If the architect needs to issue a variation, he should not do this informally and on site at the time of his inspections. Variations need to be given in accordance with the terms of the contract as they have implications on the date of practical completion of the project and possible claims for additional monies from the contractor.

If you have not employed an architect and are carrying out the site inspections on your own, it would be prudent to have some procedure to follow each time you inspect the works, rather than to approach the inspections in an ad hoc manner. These checklists are too extensive to reproduce here, and can be found in texts dedicated to project and contract administration.

The architect may also wish to open up the works and test various materials to ensure that they are in accordance with the contract. You should be aware that if the works are found to be in accordance with the contract, the contractor is entitled to additional time and money to complete the works.

Health and safety

Construction sites are notoriously dangerous places to work. There are laws to ensure that all workplaces are safe and healthy working environments. You are likely to have seen advisory posters in your workplace referring to the Health and Safety at Work Act 1974. Construction is inherently more dangerous than most working environments, so legislation was introduced specifically for construction

projects. These rules are set out in the Construction (Design and Management) Regulations 1994.

The act was introduced to ensure that a safe site is managed and that safe construction methods are incorporated. For most domestic projects the responsibilities for complying with the act rests with your professionals. If the works are not domestic and the project will last longer than 30 days or will involve more than 500 person days of construction work, the project is notifiable to the Heath and Safety Executive (HSE).

Notification to the HSE takes the form of a simple statement that sets out the following details:

● Exact address of the construction site.

● Name and address of the client and contractor.

● Type of project.

● Name and address of the planning supervisor (where applicable)

● A declaration from the planning supervisor that he has been appointed as such.

● Date that the construction phase is due to start and its intended duration.

● Estimated maximum number of people working on site.

● Planned number of contractors on site.

If the project is not notifiable and the largest number of people carrying out construction work at any one time at the site is less than five, the regulations that need to be complied with are further watered down. In such instances the only responsibility is upon the designer to ensure that the designs for the works are suitable to minimise any health and safety risks on site, adequately protect those working on site, and contain adequate health and safety information with respect to materials used.

It is useful to browse the Health and Safety Executive's website. They also produce a free leaflet setting out what health and safety considerations need to be taken into account for those undertaking works to their homes.

Liability to visitors and trespassers

As the owner of a property or building site, you have a responsibility to ensure the safety of visitors to, and, to a certain extent, trespassers on your site. If you fail to ensure their safety you may expose yourself to a claim in damages. There are two issues; the first a responsibility to visitors and the second a responsibility to trespassers.

In the case of visitors the law is set out in the Occupiers Liability Act 1957. This act provides for a duty of care to be owed by the occupier of a premises to any visitor. Who is an occupier is a question of degree. If you have handed over the plot of land to a design-and-build contractor, it will be the contractor who would owe the visitor a duty of care. Conversely, if you have a kitchen fitter installing a new kitchen in your existing house while you are occupying it, you are likely to be regarded as the occupier.

A visitor need not be someone who you have expressly invited onto the premises. It is conceivable that a visitor could be someone who believes they have an implied right to be on your land. People who use public rights of way are not considered visitors, but you do owe them the same duty of care that you would owe a trespasser.

It is unlikely that you would be held liable for any injuries that a visitor sustains if:

● You have warned a visitor not to go onto the site or an area of it.

Case study

Joy, a five-year-old girl, went for a walk in a public park, which was under the control of a corporation. Joy picked some big purple berries from a shrub – these were poisonous although they looked like blackcurrants and were understandably alluring to children. The corporation was aware of the poisonous nature of the berries, but did not adequately fence the shrub, nor did it display any warnings. Joy had no right to approach the shrub, nor did she have a right to pick the berries, but the fact that she was a child allured by berries was sufficient for the corporation to be liable.

● The visitor goes to an area of the site to which you would not reasonably expect him to go.

You should be aware that an occupier owes a greater duty of care to children than they would to adults – it is the more adventurous nature of children that imposes this higher standard of care.

To relieve yourself of liability you must take reasonable steps to sufficiently and adequately warn visitors of dangers, and to take reasonable steps so that they are safe. Liability will not be discharged if the notice is unreadable or not in an obvious place.

Your liability is discharged if the injuries are caused by the negligence of a contractor that has sufficient control of the site. In this scenario your responsibility is going to be limited to ensuring that the contractor was competent to carry out the works and manage the site. If you are undertaking a large project, your liability to a visitor may only be discharged if you employed a suitable professional to both manage the site and the contractor. It will be a question of degree as to what steps you need to take to ensure a safe site.

If the visitor acted in such a way that he contributed to his injuries, any award will be reduced. The courts regard this as being contributory negligence. A simple example is where car X went into the back of car Y and the occupants of car Y did not wear seat belts. Any award to the occupants of car Y will be reduced, as by not wearing seatbelts they contributed to the extent of their injuries.

Any warning sign that you do erect cannot exclude liability for death or personal injury for negligence.

The rights of trespassers are governed by legislation. The rules that set out an occupier's responsibility to trespassers are set out in the Occupiers Liability Act 1984. You (as the occupier) owe a duty of care to a trespasser if:

● You are aware of a danger or have reasonable grounds to believe that a danger exists.

● You know or reasonably believe that there are trespassers in the vicinity of the danger or that they may come into the vicinity of the danger.

● The risk is one against which, in all the circumstances of the case, you may reasonably expect to offer some protection. An obvious example is a building site in or near a populated area.

The duty owed to the trespasser is to take all reasonable steps to ensure that they do not suffer any injury by reason of the danger that is posed. You should warn of the dangers and take practical steps to prevent entry to the site. Clearly if you have a persistent trespasser who ignores your warnings, climbs the fence and then injuries himself, your liability may well, in the eyes of the court, be discharged.

Managing the contract
Instructions and variations
Despite having all the drawings in place, unforeseen difficulties may require the architect to issue a formal instruction to vary the scope of the works. Most

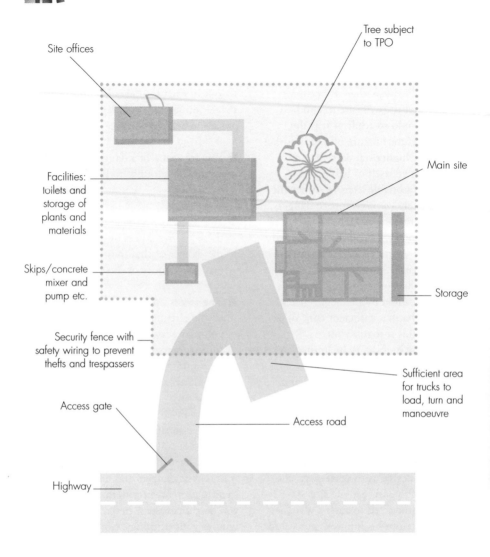

Site offices

Tree subject to TPO

Facilities: toilets and storage of plants and materials

Main site

Skips/concrete mixer and pump etc.

Storage

Security fence with safety wiring to prevent thefts and trespassers

Sufficient area for trucks to load, turn and manoeuvre

Access gate

Access road

Highway

CONSIDER:
- Site safety
- Site huts – workers, canteen, foreman etc
- Hoarding/security
- General plant – dumpers, mixers, cranes, scaffolding
- Storage areas – open, covered, locked, special (thermal/insulation)

Site plan.

standard building contracts have a mechanism for the manner in which an instruction is issued to the contractor; it would be prudent to check that this is the case with respect to your individual building contract.

Instructions issued by the architect must usually be made in writing. If they are given orally, they must be confirmed (usually within a week) in writing to the contractor. The effective date of an instruction is the date that it is issued. All instructions should follow a standard form produced by RIBA or another professional organisation. It pays dividends to pay attention to the details of any instruction so that they are clear and can be complied with without any confusion.

A contractor usually has an opportunity to object to an instruction. Most contracts set out that any such objection is made in writing, with reasons, and within a set time frame.

Additional works (or omissions) should be valued on the basis of the bills of quantities. If this is not possible, the works should be valued on a daywork basis. If neither of these are possible, a fair valuation must be made.

It is possible for a variation to have a knock-on effect on the nature and scope of the future works. In these cases, the change should also be considered as a variation. However, as you can imagine this is a grey area, and varies for each project and the variations issued within it.

Cost management

Many of the best-planned projects run over time and over budget. With respect to the time factor, we have already seen that an allocation of a float of a few days in the programme is advisable. It would also be wise to have a contingency sum to account for additional costs.

You can keep your costs down by careful planning at the pre-tender stage so that you are clear in your mind what the scope of your project is. This will minimise any changes in the design and materials which you may have otherwise have made. Contractors don't tend to like changes and can price harshly. I suggest keeping a monthly tab on costing to ensure that all is going to plan.

Interim certificates

An interim certificate is the trade name given to the monthly payment made by the employer to the contractor. Traditionally, the interim certificate is prepared by the architect, based upon the value of the work done on the date of the interim certificate. However, you may have agreed a different payment mechanism with your contractor.

The mechanism of issuing an interim certificate is for the architect to inspect and value the works and then to issue an interim certificate to the employer, who then has usually 14 or 21 days to pay the contractor this sum of money. It is also possible for the quantity surveyor to prepare the interim certificates. The contract sum should be exclusive of VAT, so VAT is excluded for the purposes of the interim valuations. It is the contractor's responsibility to separately bill the employer for any VAT. If your works are either exempt or at a reduced rate, your quantity surveyor or architect will assist. Again, all the professional organisations (text continues on page 106)

Timescale (days)

ACTIVITY		2	4	6	8	10	12	14	16	18	20
Move in and set out	A	█									
Clear and level site	B		█	█							
Excavate for drain	Q					█					
Lay concrete and pipes for drain	R						█	█			
Backfill to drain	S									█	
Excavate foundations	C				█						
Formwork & reinforcement in foundations	D						█	█	█	█	█
Concrete in foundations	E							█	█		
Backfill around foundations	F								█		
Hardcore under floor slab	G									█	
Concrete in slab	H										█
Curing of foundations	J										
Delivery of portal frames	K										
Erect steel portal frames	L										
Brick external cladding	M										
Roof cladding	N										
Gutters etc.	P										
Glaze and external paint	T										
Internal decorations	U										
Clean away	V										

KEY

Drainage works

Preliminaries

 Foundations to ground level work

 Ground level to roof and decorating works

Timescale (days)

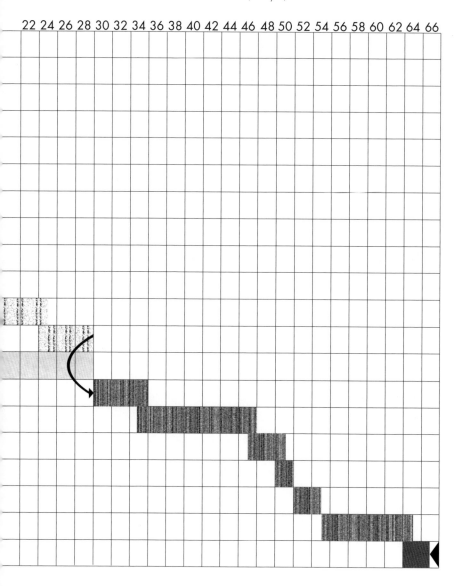

Programming the works.

(including RIBA) produce forms to be used as interim certificates. If you propose to withold monies that are properly due to the contractor then you must issue the contractor with a witholding notice. A witholding notice must usually be issued within five days of the contractor's invoice; it must state the amount of monies witheld and why (for example, poor workmanship).

The final account tends to occur within six months of practical completion. The final account is evidence that all monies have been paid – and not that the works have been completed to a satisfactory standard, as some contractors try to argue. In assessing the final account the contractor sends all the paperwork required to prepare the final account to the architect/quantity surveyor, including things such as claims for loss and expense. The architect and quantity surveyor take these factors into account and issue the final account and final certificate for payment at the end of the defects liability period.

KEY POINTS

● Communication and teamwork are critical to ensure a successful project.

● Give careful thought to how you will run the site in a safe manner.

● You should have an idea of how to manage the contract, but it may be wise to pass this responsibility onto a professional.

● The contract is a guide as to how to run the project – it is not a document to be referred to only when things go wrong.

CHAPTER 10

Consumer Rights

Life is not perfect, and it could well be that you have not entered into a written contract with your architect, contractor or supplier. If you have a dispute, they may try and pull the wool over your eyes with something along the lines of "Oral contract, not worth the paper it's written on, mate." Fortunately, there is protection for consumers. A basic minimum with respect to the quality of services, goods and materials used is implied in all consumer contracts for the sale of goods and supply of services.

Sale of Goods Act 1979

The Sale of Goods Act implies certain terms into most consumer contracts. Under the act, the buyer (you) can expect that the goods supplied will meet the following criteria:

● **Goods to conform with their description**
Where you have purchased goods based upon a description provided by the seller, you are entitled to rely upon the goods conforming to that same description. If you have sampled a selection of the goods (such as a paint sample), it is not sufficient if only the bulk of the goods match the sample.

● **Goods are of a satisfactory quality**
What constitutes a satisfactory quality depends upon what a reasonable person would regard as being satisfactory, taking into account factors such as:

● the cost and description of the goods.

● subjective factors, such as pride in the appearance of the goods.

● warnings, instructions and actions which need to be taken in conjunction with the use, or setting up, of the goods.

● packaging of the goods (even if the goods themselves are of satisfactory quality).

● the absence of hidden defects.

● the goods are both sufficiently durable and capable of maintaining their quality for a reasonable period of time.

● **The state and condition of the goods**
The goods must be:

● fit for the purpose for which they are commonly supplied.

● free from minor defects.

● safe, durable and of suitable appearance and finish.

You must, however, be careful, because the seller can wriggle out of a few of these provisions – for example, if you examine the goods in such a manner that would normally reveal a defect, or if the seller tells you of certain defects at the time of the purchase.

The key provision, as most contractors will tell you, is fitness for purpose. If you buy oak beams to use for your timber frame, you expect those oak beams to be fit for their intended use. How do you ensure that the seller will not brush off your complaint when you realise that the oak beams are not going to be fit for use in the timber frame? You must tell the seller what you are intending to use the product for. As always, it is best to put this in writing.

Time and money

If the contract does not provide for either a price for the goods or the time frame within which the goods are to be delivered, the act ensures that the buyer must pay the seller a reasonable price and that the goods must be delivered within a reasonable time. This provision tends to work in the seller's favour, so it is best for you to agree, in writing, the cost and delivery time for the goods.

Problems specific to house builders

The Sale of Goods Act applies to everything from the compact disc player that you bought for Christmas to the carpet you are going to lay in your new house.

House building has its own special problems. For example, you may not know whether those oak beams are fit for the purpose until you have completed the timber structure and notice that they cannot take the load. The goods are now fixed and you cannot "reject" them. This point is not new, and the act still protects you, even where there is a mixed element of purchasing the goods and carrying out works to them.

Supply of Goods and Services Act 1982

As with the Sale of Goods Act, Parliament has ensured that certain terms are implied into a contract for the supply of services. Where a contractor or a professional is carrying out services, the following terms are implied into the contract:

● The contractor or professional must carry out the works with reasonable skill and care.

● If the fees have not been agreed, the contractor is entitled to be paid a reasonable amount for those services.

● If the timescale for the performance of the services has not been agreed, the contractor must complete his works within a reasonable timescale.

Clearly it is in your interests to agree, in writing, the fees and timescale for the performance of the services as what may be considered reasonable is arbitrary.

Can the acts be excluded?

Sellers and suppliers of services may try to expressly exclude the terms of both acts and thus remove your rights to these basic minima. This should always be resisted. Whether they can or cannot exclude the terms is an entire area of law itself, but if such an exclusion has not been made clear to you, or if it is not obvious at the time of signing the contract, chances are that the exclusion is invalid.

Faulty goods

If the goods purchased for the construction of your home do not conform to the above minimum requirements, you may be entitled to one of three basic remedies. You may:

- Reject the goods and obtain a refund.

- Claim for damages.

- Insist that the seller completes their part of the deal (known in the legal trade as "specific performance").

First steps
You must be able to show some form of evidence that you have purchased the goods from the seller within the last six years. This need not be a receipt – a suitable bank/credit card statement will do.

The supplier is wrong if he insists that your claim is against the manufacturer. The law provides that your rights are against the supplier of the goods. Any guarantees provided with the goods are in addition to these statutory rights. For example, many shops will state that you can return the goods within 14 days for a refund or exchange etc. These rights are in addition to your rights under the Sale of Goods and Supply of Services Acts. When shop notices state that their exchange or return policies for goods sold do not affect your statutory rights, what they are really saying is that your rights (set out above) under the sale of goods and supply of services acts are not affected.

Finally, any sign saying "No Refunds" is an offence and should be reported to your local Trading Standards Department.

Rejecting goods
You are only entitled to reject goods if you have not accepted them. Rejecting goods amounts to returning the goods to the seller and obtaining a full refund.

What amounts to accepting the goods? You, the purchaser, are deemed to have accepted the goods if you have:

- Indicated to the seller that you have accepted them.

- Acted in a manner that would suggest that you own the goods.

- Retained the goods for a "lengthy" period of time.

Indicating acceptance to the seller
Purchasing the goods after having given them a comprehensive examination, or telling the seller that you are accepting the goods as your own may be examples of where you have indicated to the seller that you have accepted the goods.

Sometimes you may take delivery of goods and materials by signing for them. The delivery sheet may even state that by signing it you are deemed to have accepted the goods (and accordingly are not entitled to reject them). This is usually wrong. You are not deemed to have accepted the goods until you have had a reasonable chance of examining them.

The law ensures that an offer of repair does not entitle the seller to assume that you have accepted the goods. If you are to have the goods repaired, ask for a substitute or the cost of hiring one until the goods are repaired.

In house building, goods may be delivered either in instalments or as a mass of goods under a single contract. If a mass of goods has been supplied under a single contract and some of the goods are defective, you are entitled to either reject the entire consignment or accept the non-defective goods and reject the rest.

Ownership of the goods

An example of an act which would suggest that you, and not the seller, own the goods is where you have used the goods as part of the house-building process and can no longer restore them to the same condition in which you purchased them.

Keeping the goods for a period of time

Finally, if you have had the goods long enough to uncover any defect, you are deemed to have accepted the goods. What constitutes a reasonable length of time depends upon the circumstances and complexity of the goods – "What would be a reasonable time in relation to a bicycle would hardly suffice for a nuclear submarine" was a guideline given by one judge!

Financial compensation

You are entitled to sue for financial compensation if you are unable to reject the goods. If you take this option, you will not be entitled to reject the goods at a later stage.

The amount you can claim is the sum of money that would put you in the position you would be in had the seller fulfilled his part of the deal. In addition to this, you may also claim for the financial loss you have incurred because you had relied upon the contract being successful.

Specific performance

A court may insist that the seller performs his part of the deal to complete the contract. However, courts tend to be reluctant to enforce this remedy. If this approach is taken, you will not be entitled to make a claim for damages for any breach of contract.

Defective services

Here, you are entitled only to damages and specific performance. Due to the nature of the breach and the available remedies, you must act with great care. First, try to communicate your concerns with the contractor, then obtain several quotes for the cost of completing (and remedying) the faulty works. Second, deduct this amount from the payments due to the contractor (or retention held). The construction contract is likely to set out the steps that you need to take when withholding monies from the contractor and the strict time limits within which these steps must be taken.

SUMMARY

Whichever remedy you decide upon, remember to be proactive in minimising your losses. When dealing with the supplier, I'd suggest being courteous. Anger tends to entrench the wrongful supplier and makes the process of remedying the situation more difficult. Nevertheless, there are always cowboys and crafty suppliers who require a stern response from a house builder, like yourself, who knows his legal rights.

Liability for dangerous products

The Consumer Protection Act 1987 protects consumers from defective products where damage is suffered as a result of using that product. A product is defective if it does not offer the standard of safety that one would normally expect of a product of that type. In establishing this, one would look at the product itself, the manner in which it is used and any supporting and advisory literature that guides the user on how to use the product.

Any party that uses the defective product and suffers some damage as a result of it can make a claim for damages. Therefore, the potential claims are not restricted to those persons that actually purchased the goods. The parties that one can sue are:

● The manufacturer of the product.

● Any person that holds himself out to be the manufacturer of the product (look at the labels etc. on the product or sale literature).

● The party that imported the product into the European Union from a country outside the European Union.

Most normal day-to-day products that are used in the construction of a home fall into the scope of the act. However, if you are using a more obscure product, you may need to refer to the act to see if it falls within its scope.

The damages that one can claim for are:

● Personal injury.

● Loss or damage to other property (for example, a defective stripper damaging otherwise suitable materials).

There are a variety of defences available to the manufacturer – one of the most obvious is that the product was not used for the purpose for which it was intended.

KEY POINTS

The Sale of Goods and Supply of Services Act implies certain terms into written and oral contracts where the parties have not considered the circumstances. The Act ensures that:

Goods that you have purchased must:

● Correspond with their description.

● Be fit for the purpose for which they are supplied.

● Be of a satisfactory quality.

● Be free from minor defects.

If the goods do not conform with the above, you may:

● Reject the goods and obtain a refund.

● Claim for damages.

● Request specific performance.

If you contracted out specialist services, then (subject to what you may have agreed in a written contract), the contractor must:

● Carry out the services with reasonable skill and care.

● Complete them within a reasonable time frame.

● Be paid a reasonable fee.

If the services do not conform with the above, you may:

● Claim for damages.

● Request specific performance.

CHAPTER 11

Negligence

Negligence (and nuisance) fall into the area of law known as tort, which can be regarded as the law that covers normal (non-contractual) human relations. Tort is an area of law that is separate from contract law. You do not need to have a contract with another person in order to bring an action in either nuisance or negligence. There is some overlap between tort and contract law, but this is outside the scope of this book.

Basics of negligence

If you think of tort as being the law that governs normal human interaction, an act of negligence is where the person that is being negligent owes the affected person a duty of care. If there is no duty of care between the parties, then even if the act is immoral or plain stupid, there is no right of action in negligence. If a duty of care is owed, and there is a breach of this duty that gives a direct rise to some form of damage, there is an actionable right in negligence for damages. There are also additional factors that need to be considered, such as contributory negligence, and intervening factors that break the chain of causation from the original act of the negligence to the ultimate damage caused.

Duty of care

Certain relationships always establish a duty of care – for example, a professional owes his client a duty of care, or the manufacturer of a product owes the consumer a duty of care.

A definition of what kind of relationship would establish a duty of care is one where the parties are so closely and directly affected that the actions of one party would require him to think about the affect and consequences of his actions or inaction.

A negligent act arises when this duty of care is broken. The duty can be broken by an action or inaction of the person that owes the duty. However, what is brought into question is the standard of care that is owed. For example, a builder owes you a duty of care in carrying out the works to your home. The standard of that care would be what one would reasonably expect from a similarly (competent) skilled and qualified builder. If you are calling into question the methods used or poor decision-making, this may merely be a question of bad judgement on the part of the professional, rather than amounting to an act of negligence.

The final hurdle is to establish loss and damage arising from the negligent act. When you consider the negligent act, you must consider each stage from that act to the damage that was suffered, and whether there were any intervening acts. These intervening acts may be caused either by the person who has suffered the damage or by an external third party. There is a grey area when trying to establish whether an intervening act would amount to either contributory negligence (and thus reduce the damages recoverable) or so unreasonable (or extreme) as to break the

Case Study

Albert's contractor was nearing the end of the construction of his new home and was completing the roof. Unfortunately, the contractor was negligent in the completion of the roof, and the following week it rained and there was some minor leakage. Albert took it upon himself to climb onto the roof and fix it. Albert, not having a clue about construction, damaged the roof even further, thus causing an even bigger leak and more damage to his property. Whether this was an act that would discharge the negligence of the contractor or simply an act of contributory negligence and reduce Albert's compensation is open to question. If, however, Albert decided to go on the roof and fix it in the middle of a storm (remember, the leak was only minor – this was not a emergency) and he slipped and fell, he would be unlikely to be able to recover for any personal injuries.

chain of causation and get the original person that caused the negligence off the hook.

In establishing the extent of the losses that are recoverable, consider what is known as the "but for" test. What this means is you ask yourself, "But for the actions of X, would Y have suffered the damage?" A second test is remoteness – if the damage is so remote as not to be reasonably foreseeable, you are unlikely to be able to recover for the damage.

Pure economic loss

There is a peculiarity in negligence that one cannot recover for pure economic loss. This area of law is complex, and an in-depth analysis of it is outside the scope of this book. An inability to recover losses where the damage caused is purely economic is common in construction disputes. If you have recently purchased a house and there is no NHBC cover and you do not have any collateral warranties from the original contractor or professionals that carried out the work, your only recourse for defective work would be in tort under negligence. Unfortunately, you are unlikely to be able to recover the costs of the repair, as this is considered to be pure economic loss.

You may have an argument to claim for pure economic loss if the negligent building work is so severe as to cause a danger to the health and safety of the occupants or third parties, and, more unusually, if the negligent work caused damage to other property. Conceptually, both lawyers and judges have over the years had a field day trying to nail down what is considered to be "other property". A possible example would be where the boiler blew up and damaged the roof of the house – the boiler is one item of property and the roof a separate

Case Study

Unsafe Roofing contractors were carrying out works to the family home of Mr and Mrs Johnson. They were surprisingly cheap in their tender, and were by far the cheapest tender of the five that Mr Johnson had sought. In addition to this, they completed the works in record time and took cash. Mr Johnson, who was not experienced in DIY matters, was trusting and did not think anything was untoward. Several weeks later there was a mild rainstorm that caused the roof to cave in during the night. This caused the electricity to be cut and put the Johnsons out of communication with the outside world. In the ensuing mayhem, Mrs Johnson broke an ankle and Mr Johnson was knocked unconscious.

Unsafe Roofing were clearly negligent.

As Mr and Mrs Johnson were famous celebrities who lived in a small village, the rescue services arrived on the scene together with an army of reporters, and television crews who filmed the whole sorry tale. The parents of Mr Johnson were watching the local news, and Mr Johnson's father, thinking that his son was critically injured, had a heart attack on hearing the news.

While *Unsafe Roofing* were negligent, it would be considered too remote for them to be liable to Mr Johnson's father for the heart attack he suffered as a consequence of their defective work.

item of property, and one should be able to recover for the damage to the roof in negligence from the manufacturer of the boiler. This area of law is horribly convoluted, and you would do well to seek professional advice.

However, what this does highlight is the importance of having some form of warranty, either in the form of a collateral warranty (a separate agreement between yourself and the contractor, giving you rights to sue the contractor under the original building contract which you were not a party to) or in the form of warranty cover from the NHBC, Zurich or other warranty provider.

KEY POINTS

● In order to bring a claim for negligence you need to establish that a duty of care was owed, that the duty was breached and some damage resulted from the breach.

● Acts of contributory negligence or an intervening act may limit the damages you can claim for a negligent act.

● You cannot normally recover for pure economic loss for negligent work. This highlights the importance of having a contractual relationship in place.

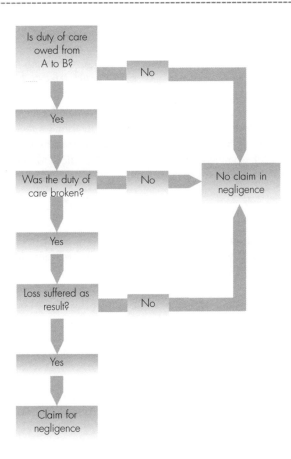

Negligence.

CHAPTER 12

Nuisance

Nuisance is a common accusation that is banded about between neighbours in relation to construction works. Whilst the law of nuisance is primarily a private one, you will recall that a person can be guilty of a public nuisance (such as a statutory nuisance). A private nuisance is a civil dispute, while a public nuisance can be a criminal act.

Nuisance can be regarded as both the law that protects our environment and the law that protects our right to the enjoyment of our land. For the purposes of this book, I will look at two types of nuisances:

● Damage to your land caused by a neighbour.

● Interference with the quiet enjoyment of your land.

For example, things that encroach onto your land, such as leakage of water, tree roots and shrubs, can be considered to be a nuisance once a certain threshold of acceptability has been exceeded. This is in addition to the more traditional concepts of what constitutes a nuisance, such as excessive noise. The law relating to nuisance is a balancing act between the right of one neighbour to use his land as he so wishes and the right of the opposing neighbour not to be inconvenienced by such use. Ascertaining when this threshold has been reached comes back to the old adage of what actions a normal person would consider reasonable (unless, of course, the nuisance has damaged your land).

Only the person who has an interest in the land can bring an action for nuisance. For example, a tenant (as opposed to a guest) and a landlord can bring an action for nuisance. The person that is sued is either the person that creates the nuisance or the occupier. This is a particular concern to those self-builders and home improvers who are carrying out construction works to their premises. If your contractor is carrying out works to your land and is generating excessive noise, dust etc. that is causing a nuisance, then you, as the occupier, are liable in an action for nuisance. However, your building contract should have a provision where the contractor will indemnify you for any nuisances that he generates or causes. This is in addition to the implied term that the contractor shall carry out the works with reasonable skill and care.

When considering the reasonableness of a noisy neighbour, there are a number of factors that are taken into consideration by the courts, such as:

● The extent of the nuisance.

● The length of time that the nuisance has been going on for.

● The character of the area.

● The intention of the parties.

● The damage caused.

The extent of the nuisance
The nuisance would generally need to be

a fairly continuous nuisance, rather than something that happens once every so often. The courts will tend to consider additional factors such as when the nuisance occurs. For example, building your conservatory at 8 am on a Sunday is not only likely to breach any planning conditions that may be in force, but is also likely to give rise to an action in nuisance by your neighbour.

If there is a breakout or escape of a nuisance from your neighbour's land to your land, this is also actionable. Normally, one-off escapes would not be considered as being actionable. However, there are certain circumstances where a

Rule of Rylands and Fletcher

Where a party keeps anything on his land that may cause some harm if it escapes, the risk for any damage caused by its escape rests with that owner.

The first step is to establish that something was brought onto the land, as opposed to it being something natural or something that would ordinarily be used in normal day-to-day activities. There must be some special use for bringing it on to the land. For example, normal use of water, gas, electricity would not give rise to an action under the rule of Rylands and Fletcher; however, bulk storage of water would.

Second, whatever is brought on to the land must "escape". This means that it must transgress from your neighbour's land (where you have no control) into your land (where you have control). It must also be capable of causing some harm. It is conceivable that water can intentionally be brought on to land, and if it escapes it is something that could cause serious harm. The crux here is that even if your neighbour took all reasonable steps to prevent the escape of whatever was brought on to the land, this would not be enough to get him off the hook, and he may still be liable for any damage caused.

Whatever escapes needs to have caused damage, and establishing what damage you could recover comes back to that which is reasonable. Any damage caused which is too remote from the action that gave rise to it is unlikely to be recoverable.

Even if you feel that you can tick off each of the above requirements, in order to bring an action within the rule of Rylands and Fletcher there are a number of defences available to your neighbour. These are: where the escape was caused by an act of god or the actions of a stranger, if your neighbour had your consent (either expressly or impliedly), or if you had a hand in the escape of the harmful substances.

single escape can amount to an action for nuisance – this is known in the legal trade as the rule of Rylands and Fletcher (see box below).

How long has the nuisance been going on for?

Much of this depends on the damage caused. If the nuisance has damaged your property, it need not have been going on for a significant amount of time. If the nuisance is something more intangible, such as noise, the courts would look to what would be reasonable – the nuisance would need to be something that materially interferes with normal day-to day comfort and habits of living. Clearly, there is a degree of interpretation here!

If your neighbour is causing the nuisance out of malice, the threshold is deceased in your favour. This means that even if the action itself is not a nuisance in the normal course of day-to-day activities, the fact that there is some malice will ensure that these actions will amount to an actionable nuisance.

The character of the area

If you're going to live in the middle of a city centre, you cannot expect the same level of serenity as if you live in the countryside. However, the test is that of a reasonable person. So if you have some sensitive plants or other property, no special consideration is given to these. Nor is special consideration given to people who are unusually sensitive to noise or smells etc.

Damage caused

You need to show that you have suffered some damage. This can either be physical damage to your property or personal damage to the enjoyment of your land.

If you are bringing an action for nuisance, or if one is being brought against you, you must be aware of certain defences that may be available. For example, if the nuisance has been going on for more than 20 years, it is unlikely that an action against it can be raised. However, there are degrees of acceptability to this general rule. It is no defence to say that someone has moved into the area where the nuisance was being committed. Other defences could be, depending upon the circumstances, acts of god and consenting to the nuisance.

Remedies

The extent of the damages that you can claim is that which would put you in the position that you would be in had the nuisance never been committed. This is not the easiest of tasks when ascertaining the damage caused to one's enjoyment of the land. Alternatively, you may push for a court injunction stopping the nuisance. Any injunction that may be awarded is at the discretion of the court and will depend upon the individual circumstances of the case.

CHAPTER 13

Resolving Disputes

Disputes are an unfortunate element of human society. Most disputes can be, and should be, resolved amicably. I tend to consider the courts a last resort option – once the legal process has begun it is very difficult to stop, on top of which there is the stress, financial impact and possible delays to your development to consider.

For most people involved in the building industry, disputes form an everyday part of business life. The likely reasons are a combination of a fragmented industry (with several parties trying to get a job done, but each having differing interests) and an infinite list of things that could go wrong with a project. Many of these things are unforeseeable at the time of starting the project, and then the finger-pointing begins as different parties presume that the risk belongs to another party.

In a simple world, the risks are clearly allocated between an employer and a contractor, but think of the risks presented by unforeseen ground conditions or a third party (such as the local authority) delaying the issuing of any licences or permits etc. The benefits of a design-and-build contract are self-evident.

The conflict of interests between the parties involved in the construction process led to such a disproportionate amount of disputes that a few years ago legislation was introduced so that construction now has its own special form of dispute resolution known as adjudication. Adjudication is a quasi-judicial form of dispute resolution which is supposed to be quick, easy and relatively cheap. For most self-build projects of residential homes, adjudication is not going to be the required form of dispute resolution. Large and complex construction disputes are even privy to their own court – the Technology and Construction Court, based in Central London.

Depending upon the nature of your dispute, it may make both commercial and practical sense not to litigate, even if this is a bitter pill to swallow. Have no illusions: most disputes are an uphill struggle with a deleterious impact on your wallet and sanity, particularly if you are planning on conducting the litigation on your own.

There are a few key questions that need to be asked before you threaten any form of action. For example, you need to ask whom are you going to sue, on what basis, for what amount of compensation and to ensure that you are not out of time in bringing the dispute – about 90 per cent of all claims are settled out of court, usually before the disclosure stage.

Who to sue?

If you are going down the traditional route of procurement and the design was faulty and you had employed an architect to do the design, the obvious answer is to sue the architect. Conversely, if the design was fine but the contractor failed to build in accordance with the design, you sue the contractor. If it was a combination of these two elements, you are likely to sue them both. If you do decide to sue them both, you need to allocate responsibility separately to each party. In a design-and-build contract the contractor is generally responsible for both the design and construction of the project.

On what basis are you going to bring the action?

This is where you try to pinpoint the breach of contract. Establishing what the terms of the contract were may be difficult if the contract was oral. There is also scope to bring an action (in tort) for negligence. However, it will generally be preferable to sue for a breach of contract. The amount of damages you can claim for is the amount that would put you in the position had the contract been properly performed.

If the terms of your contract are unclear or it was an oral contract, there is no need to panic. The Sale of Goods and Supply of Services Acts imply certain terms into all contracts where a professional service is provided, and imply that a professional will use reasonable skill and care in carrying out the services, and will use suitable materials.

If you establish that a (valid) contract was established and its terms were breached, consider whether you are out of time in bringing the claim. For contracts that are signed "underhand", with just the names of the parties signed on the execution clause, you have six years within which to bring a claim. If the contract is signed as a deed, this is extended to 12 years. For a contract to be signed as a deed, it must be clear that the parties intended the contract to be a deed and that it is signed as a deed. This

means that the execution clause will state something like "Signed by X as a deed".

If you have a valid contract which has been breached and you have suffered some loss, consider the level of compensation that you may be entitled to. For a breach of contract, the basic level of compensation that you are entitled to is the sum of money that would put you in the position had the contract been properly performed.

Alternative remedies

There are other remedies for a breach of contract, such as specific performance, which is where the court can compel the other party to complete their part of the contract. This remedy is rarely used by the courts, and if you have lost faith in the contractor's work, it is academic.

There is no reason why you cannot sue one or all of the professionals you have employed, provided that you can show that there is a valid contract, a breach of the contract (for each professional/contractor) and that you have suffered some loss.

There is a responsibility on you to mitigate any losses that you incur as a consequence of the breach of contract by the other party. For example, if a piling sub-contractor walks off site, and as a consequence you are losing money because the timber frame subcontractor you have employed cannot commence his works, then you should employ another piling subcontractor to complete the works and minimise your losses. Mitigating your losses is critical. If you do not mitigate your losses, you will substantially reduce the amount of money recoverable. You should inform the other party that if they fail to remedy their breach you will do whatever is necessary to mitigate your loss, and that they will be liable for those costs.

Tort

As we have already discussed, you do not always need to establish the existence of a contract in order to sue another party; there is also a right of action in what is known as the law of tort. For most building disputes it allows you to sue professionals if their work is negligent.

You need to establish that they owe you a duty of care, that this duty was broken, and that you suffered a loss. The compensation provisions here are different, and the sum of money that you could get is the sum that would put you in the position you would have been in had the professional never been negligent.

If you decide to go down this route, I strongly advise getting professional advice, as there is a legal complexity in that the person making the claim cannot recover for purely economic losses. The time limit for bringing an action is generally six years from the date that the tort is committed (but can be as short as three years) and in certain cases the trigger is six years from the date that the damage happened.

In tort, the courts look to see whether there is any contributory negligence – this is where your actions may have partly contributed to your loss. If this is the case, any damages awarded will be reduced accordingly.

Viability of the claim

While you may be in the right, there is

little point in bringing an action against an insolvent company or a bankrupt person; the chances of you recovering an award that may be made in your favour are minimal. You must also be sure that you can locate the party you are intending to sue. A company will have a registered address, but a sole trader may just have a PO box and a mobile telephone number.

It is worth pointing out that most contractors, architects and other professionals have insurance. If you have used a contract, it is likely that it requires them to maintain either professional indemnity insurance (for negligent design work), public liability insurance (if their works injure a third party) or contractor's all-risks insurance (usually limited to those listed in the policy). It may be that architects and other professionals operating under the umbrella of their professional organisation are required to maintain insurance by virtue of their membership. By going straight to the insurers you may be able to negotiate a quicker and less painful settlement than bringing an action through the courts. However, you may well need to kick-start the litigation process in order to push the insurers to act.

If you decide that you have all the requisite elements to bring a claim, the next step is to consider the forum that you will try to settle the dispute. Forums rank in severity and complexity from simple negotiations to full-scale court actions. The main choices of forums are:

● Negotiation (not strictly a forum, but must be considered before launching into any court action).

● Mediation and conciliation.

● Arbitration – this is no longer the forum of choice for many claimants, it can actually be more expensive and take longer than a court action. Its main advantage is that the dispute is kept private. The parties can also select their own arbitrator who is experienced in the field to which the dispute relates.

● Court: Small Claims "Court", County Court and High Court.

Presenting your claim and the forums for dispute resolution

Going to court is, in my opinion, a last resort. You should try to negotiate a settlement, but there may be instances where you are left with no choice but to resort to the courts.

Whether you are bringing a claim in court or preparing your documents pursuant to a mediation, there is a process that you should use when preparing your case. It is imperative that your case is presented in a clear, concise manner. Present only the facts; do not

---

SUMMARY

Making a claim is not to be taken lightly. Always try to resolve your dispute amicably. Keep in mind that your goal is to get your house built on time, to specification and on budget – try not to get bogged down in finger-pointing exercises on matters of principle, particularly if you have doubts as to the strength of your case. Unless the claim is straightforward (like a debt claim), it may make greater commercial sense to negotiate a settlement and accept a loss; rather than pursuing the claim and opening a potential Pandora's box. The approach to take will differ for each dispute.

KEY POINTS

● Establish that you have a valid contract, that it has been breached and that you have suffered a loss. Check to make sure that you are not out of time in making a claim.

● Consider negotiating a settlement rather than going full steam ahead to court. It may make greater commercial sense to negotiate a settlement and accept a loss if it means that the house or extension will be completed on time, to specification and on budget.

● Claims for negligence are more complex than breach of contract and specialist advice must be sought, as the compensation provisions for building disputes are complex in that you cannot recover for pure economic loss.

pepper your case with personal woes. Each fact that you assert must be backed up by evidence, which consists of things like photographs, minutes of meetings, invoices, telephone notes, letters and even statements from third parties.

When preparing your case, you should also consider whether there have been any instances where you have not mitigated your losses, or if you have contributed to the negligence of the contractor/professional and made a bad situation worse.

One of the first things to do before preparing your case is to consider the strengths and weaknesses of your case. You can do this by preparing a chart of the good facts and bad facts relating to the dispute. You should also carry out a cost/benefit analysis of your case. Consider how much the litigation is likely to cost and how much you are likely to recover. Factor into this your legal costs and those of the defendant should you lose.

When you prepare your case, you should set out its key points. For example, if it is a breach of contract you will need to establish that:

● There was a valid contract between yourself (the claimant) and the party you are suing (the defendant).

● There was a breach of its terms (express or implied).

● There was a loss suffered by you.

● You are not out of time in bringing the claim.

To show that there was a valid contract you will need to present a copy of the signed and dated contract between yourself and the party you are suing. You will then refer to the terms of the contract – for example, the contract may provide that the project should be completed by a certain date. You need to evidence the breach – if it is a case of faulty workmanship, use photos and possibly instruct an expert to provide his opinion. If there are documents that the defendant has, you can write to him requesting that copies of these are disclosed to you – this process is called disclosure (it used to be called discovery).

Disclosure must take place after pleadings are exchanged. This is usually a good stage to consider settling the dispute, especially if the other side have documents that are detrimental to their case. Both you and your opponent must show all the documents that are relevant to your case, irrespective of whether they are positive or negative. You will also need to prepare a list of all your documents. Disclosure is an expensive and time-consuming process.

Finally, establish that you are within the 6- or 12-year period within which to bring your claim and calculate your losses, which for a breach of contract is to place you in the position that you would have been in had the contract been properly performed.

Once you have prepared your written case and cross-referred it to your evidence, I suggest taking stock of the merits of your case before you submit any claim to the courts. Preparing your case in this way will also greatly assist you in any negotiations, as it will crystallise your case in your own mind.

As there may be several parties that you wish to sue, you may make a request to the court to join all these parties in a single action. If you intend to do this, there are a few ground rules:

- The cases must be pending in the same County Court or division of the High Court.

- There must be common facts (or issues of law) in each instance.

- The claim must arise out of the same facts.

- It would be beneficial and desirable to consolidate the actions.

If you do decide to bring a court action, you should consider the possibility of a counter-claim by the defendant (presuming that he has grounds for one) and the time and energy taken up in pursuing a claim in the courts. However, courts tend to take a dim view of parties that have not attempted to negotiate a settlement before bringing their case to court, and judges can express this by limiting any costs awarded to the winning party.

Before submitting any claim you need to send the defendant a "letter before action", which sets out in detail the essence of your claim and invites a settlement. Refer to the various pre-action protocols which set out the format for a letter before action. The pre-action protocols are available free from the Lord Chancellor's website.

Experts can be used to assist you in your claim. It is possible for both parties to appoint a single joint expert, and this is also the court's preferred option. However, the primary duty of any expert is to the court.

Negotiating a settlement

The circumstances of each case differ; however, there are some basic negotiating principles that should be considered. The first thing to do is ensure that all your correspondence is marked "Without Prejudice". This is to prevent the correspondence that you have written in an attempt to bring a settlement being used in the event of the matter going to trial. If the correspondence is sensitive, also mark it as being "Private and Confidential".

I do not believe that negotiations should follow the format of two parties at opposite poles, chipping away at each other until a settlement is reached. It is inevitable that the parties will both feel that they have lost and that the other party got one up on them.

You should adopt a more flexible approach. Consider what common ground both you and the professional/contractor have. For example, you both want to complete the project and be proud of your house or extension; you also want a motivated contractor and this comes from his being paid fairly and on time, and your giving him a project he can be proud of. You both need to be able to trust each other and adopt a non-aggressive stance in order to reach a settlement that both parties will consider fair.

Before you sit down with the

contractor, think of where you are going to discuss the issues – on site or somewhere more formal. Think about when you are going to speak to him – Monday morning and Friday afternoon generate very different negotiating atmospheres. Consider carefully the issues that you are going to discuss, and ensure that you do not get sidetracked into pointless bickering or allocating blame onto third parties that are not there to represent themselves.

When negotiating, be as objective as possible and keep focused on the issues at hand. Settlements do not need to be solely about money; think of other options, such as additional works that were not part of the original tender, different high-spec materials etc. When you reach a settlement, note down what was agreed. This is critical if relationships become unstuck further down the line.

Mediation and conciliation

The process of dispute resolution is not too dissimilar to negotiating. What you have is a third party (a mediator) who manages the negotiations. You need to prepare your case and present it to the mediator. Here, it pays to think and plan carefully and objectively what the breach is and what you are claiming for. A concise and crisp presentation of your position will assist you greatly. It is a prerequisite that both parties approach a mediation willingly. As with negotiations, all documents should be made on a "Without Prejudice" basis. Courts are very keen that some form of mediation is undertaken in order to settle the litigation. Mediation can be undertaken once pleadings have been

entered, and in such scenarios the courts will adjourn the proceedings so that negotiations can continue.

Mediation should be informal. The mediator will tend to look at the common ground between the parties and will try to find a win-win solution. What this means is that the mediator is not going to allocate blame, but is going to see how to take things forward as fairly as possible so that both parties feel they have won a fair compromise. The speed within which a dispute can be resolved by mediation is a lot faster than either litigation or even arbitration.

With both mediation and conciliation, both parties must be prepared to sit down and talk. If the relationships have deteriorated to the extent that you are both at each other's throats, neither of these forums are going to help.

To find a mediator you can contact one of the professional bodies on pages 170–171 or one of the dedicated mediating organisations such as CEDR (Centre for Dispute Resolution). Having conducted several mediations in the past as a mediator, I have found that where parties are willing to work together, the result is overwhelmingly positive.

There are times, however, when mediation is not going to be the best dispute resolution forum. For example, if you have a straightforward debt claim, it would be more beneficial to attain a summary judgement through the courts.

Adjudication

Most domestic self-build projects leapfrog this stage and go straight to arbitration or court. Adjudication is statutory because Parliament has set out in law that disputes arising out of construction contracts (save for a few exceptions) entered into after 1 May 1998 should, in the first instance, be resolved by adjudication. A party can refer a dispute to adjudication at any time. The rules by which this quasi-judicial process is managed are either set out in the contract or by the government in its scheme for construction contracts.

The adjudicator is either appointed in accordance with the contract or by a nominating body – for example, the Chartered Institute of Building and the Construction Industry Council are nominating bodies. The adjudicator could be a builder, architect, lawyer or surveyor.

The aim of adjudication is to give a speedy (interim) resolution of the dispute so that the works can continue with the minimum of disruption. There is always scope to appeal any decision in court at a later stage.

Typically, the party initiating the dispute (referring party) sends a notice to the other side (responding party), setting out the nature of the dispute. The responding party generally has seven days to prepare its defence (response). The time scales will vary depending upon which adjudication rules apply.

If you are making the claim, you must ensure that in preparing the notice you set out the facts of your version of events in a clear, concise and chronological manner. You must also back up each statement of fact with some form of evidence, even if this is just a signed statement (affidavit) from a colleague who can back up your claim. This is where the importance of keeping telephone notes, letters and receipts becomes imperative – it is usually the strength of these that makes or breaks your claim.

If you have received a claim (you are the defendant), you must dismantle each element of the statements that make up the claim. You do this by examining each statement and submitting the counter-arguments that offer your version of events. Each argument you present should be based on fact and be backed up with suitable evidence.

Most adjudications are based solely on written evidence, but sometimes the adjudicator may suggest an oral hearing. This sounds formal, but the format is more like an official meeting than a court proceeding.

In dealing with the dispute the adjudicator must act fairly and be seen to be acting fairly; so phone calls without the other party present are generally not acceptable. However, the nature of an adjudication is that the adjudicator may take a pro-active approach in establishing the facts and the law. He may therefore take an inquisitorial approach or leave it for both parties to make the representations.

Unfortunately, the adjudication process is not perfect. Common practice has shown that because a notice can be issued at any time, some parties use this as a tactic and serve the notice around crucial dates (such as Christmas), thus limiting the ability of the responding party to put together his response within the required time frame.

The other defect with the adjudication process tends to be that the adjudicator, in giving his decision, does not need to give reasons for it. This can cause difficulties if you still feel aggrieved and wish to resolve the dispute either in court or in arbitration.

Enforcement

Each party must abide by the decision reached by the adjudicator – but this does not always happen. In such a scenario and on the basis of the adjudicator's decision, the aggrieved party can obtain a court order forcing the non-complying party to act.

Valid arguments for resisting enforcement are that the adjudicator acted outside his brief in hearing the matter, that there was a manifest error in his decision, or that there was a breach of the rules of natural justice (or other procedural rules).

Surprisingly, many parties accept the adjudicator's decision as final, even if they disagree with it in fact or in law. There is no doubt that fewer construction disputes now go through the courts.

Bringing a claim in court

The type of court within which you bring your claim depends upon the value and complexity of your claim. Generally, for claims below £5,000 consider the Small Claims Procedure of the County Court. Between £5,000 and £25,000 bring your claim in the County Court, and above £50,000 the High Court. Claims between £25,000 and £50,000 may be brought in either the County or High Courts. Claims brought in the High Court are outside the scope of this book.

Pre-action protocol

The courts have set out a pre-action protocol that should be followed before a construction claim is submitted to the courts. This protocol is available free from the Lord Chancellor's Department's website.

The aim of the protocol is to:

● Encourage the early exchange of information in relation to the claim.

● Promote a negotiated settlement.

● Support the management of the dispute resolution process.

The party bringing the claim will need to send a letter to the proposed defendant setting out the facts of his claim, the nature of the relief claimed (such as damages or specific performance) and the names of any experts that may be used. In turn the defendant should acknowledge the claim within 14 days and give details of his insurers. The defendant must raise any objections in relation to the letter before action within 28 days of receiving the letter before action.

As soon as possible after the defendant's response, the parties should attempt to meet and negotiate a settlement. The aim of this meeting is to narrow down and focus upon the main areas of disagreement and how it could be resolved without recourse to litigation.

The County Court

The first step is to consider which is your local County Court. You can locate this on the internet at the County Court Service website (see page 170). Once you have established this, obtain claim form N1 from the Court, which is free. You should be aware that under certain circumstances your claim may be transferred to a different County Court – one of the most common reasons for this is if the defendant resides or carries on business in another County Court's area.

If you are bringing the claim, you are the claimant, and you need to prepare a copy of the N1 form for each defendant and the court. The form is fairly straightforward, but you must consider which parties you are going to sue, on what grounds and for what amount of compensation.

As already mentioned, consider, on an objective and factual basis, the strength of your case. Even if you have a strong case, you must ensure that the company you are proposing to sue is not insolvent – a quick check at Companies House will answer this (see page 170). If it is an individual, check to make sure that he is not bankrupt by calling the High Court.

Finally, consider the expense of going to court. If you are conducting the case on your own, the costs will be limited to the court fees and your time. If the case is complex, you may have to pay for building experts to give evidence on your behalf. If you lose, you may have to pay a proportion of the defendant's costs; conversely, if you win, the defendant may have to pay a proportion of your costs.

Small Claims Procedure

This is the dispute forum that you are most likely to use without specialist help. The small claims procedure is part of the County Court, it is for claims of less than £5,000, and thus is generally used for day-to-day consumer disputes.

It is unlikely that you need to physically attend court; however, you need to prepare your claim diligently. The judge may require a date for a hearing; however, there is flexibility in relation to arranging a convenient date for attending court.

If you feel that you need an expert to help you set out your claim, you may do so, providing the judge consents. The expert will need to be aware that his primary duty is to the court and not to you. It may be that the judge will require both parties to appoint a single joint expert. This may seem odd, but when you consider that the expert's overall duty is again to the court and not the individuals, the logic is clear.

If you win, there are limited costs that you can claim from the losing party, the key elements of which are:

● Court fees that have been paid.

● A maximum of £200 for an expert (approved by the judge).

● A maximum of £50 for you and any witnesses you have used for attending court, plus additional travelling and overnight costs.

Before submitting the claim, you must prepare all your evidence in a logical (usually chronological) manner. This will include collating things like receipts, contracts, telephone notes and witness statements – the items that constitute your evidence.

Diligent preparation of the documents pertaining to your case will assist you when setting out your claim. It will also allow you to assess the strength of your case from an objective and factual perspective. Finally, the judge may require you to send copies of the documents that you are relying upon to him and the defendant.

Most cases are likely to be dealt with on written representations only. Therefore, clarity in expressing the facts of your case and excellent presentation of the documentary evidence are key factors. Remember that the judge knows nothing about your case and you must present him with your facts (backed up by evidence), clearly, concisely and convincingly. Use a lever arch file with numbered tabs, and refer to each exhibit in your claim evidencing the events making up your claim. This is why I suggest presenting your case and the exhibits in a chronological manner, as there is a natural flow. Do not enclose originals (but keep them filed and available), and send only copies of receipts, contracts etc.

If the bundle is not presented in a logical manner and does not flow naturally from your statement of case, you are unlikely to endear the judge to your point of view, not a good starting point.

Finally, keep copies of everything that you send to court.

SUMMARY

Provided that the relationships have not deteriorated too far, you should always try to negotiate a settlement or involve a third party to mediate the dispute. Going to court should be a last option. What is presented here is a very simplistic overview of the court procedures – the depth of bringing a claim in the County and High Courts is beyond the scope of this book, and I strongly suggest getting expert advice which is specific to your case.

The courts are there for everyone; they are not exclusive to lawyers. Legal advice is expensive, but the small claims procedures are straightforward. Contact your local Citizens Advice Bureau. Any self builder who has the competence to construct his own home has the capacity to effectively deal with errant contractors and suppliers in a Small Claims Court.

CHAPTER 14

Sale of Property

Many home builders and home improvers are unlikely to want to sell their home immediately after spending many man-hours in carrying out hard mental and physical labour in building or improving it. Conversely, some may be building the home or renovating it precisely for the purpose of selling it on. This chapter looks at the considerations a seller needs to take into account when selling the completed property.

Key considerations

The key factors that any legal advisor worth his salt will be looking for are to ensure that:

● All planning consents have been complied with.

● Building regulations approval has been issued.

● A warranty from the builders and professionals.

If any one of these items is not in place, it is very unlikely that you will be able to sell the premises. Not only will the buyer not be prepared to take the risk, but he is unlikely to find a mortgage lender that will lend money for the purchase.

The first two items are things that you should be doing anyway, whether you intend on living in the home or if you plan to sell it. The third item – obtaining warranties – is highly advisable. Very few people can categorically state that they will live in their home for the next 12 years – it may be your intention but circumstances change, so getting warranties is prudent.

Warranties

The most common warranties for house builders are the schemes offered by the NHBC, Zurich and other providers. These are covered in detail in Chapter 2 (see pages 11–25). Other forms of warranty are called collateral warranties. These are obtained in favour of the purchaser from the original builders and professionals, warranting their performance under their appointments or, where appropriate, the building contract. If there are no underlying appointments or building contracts, the value of a warranty is going to be questionable.

Without having some form of warranty in place, it will be virtually impossible to sell your home; the exceptions to this may be where you have carried out very minor (non-structural) works.

As a seller you will need to complete a seller's property information form. This presents you with a series of questions in relation to the works carried out to the property, the consents obtained and whether you have had any disputes with your neighbours. It is critical that you are honest, as making false representations could land you in hot water.

Fixtures and fittings

You also need to give careful thought as to what fixtures and fittings you intend to sell with the property. You normally fill out a fixtures and fittings form so that both parties are clear in their mind what items are staying and which are going.

Fixtures are things that are attached to the property and form a part of the land. Therefore, they are things that you, as the seller, cannot simply remove unless you expressly provide for it in your sale and purchase contract. The types of things that fall into the category of fixtures are things like large garden ornaments that are "fixed to the land"; however, the courts have decided that garden ornaments can be considered to be fittings!

Fittings are the moveable items, things like carpets, furniture and curtains. Traditionally, fittings are the type of things that a buyer is not entitled to in the sale and purchase transactions, and is only entitled to them if the seller expressly agrees to it.

As there is a grey area as to what constitutes fixtures and fittings, the contract not only lists them but also entitles the buyer to compensation if the seller decides that he wishes to remove any fixtures. The contract will price those fittings that are to remain, ensure that they are free of any encumbrances (for example, hire-purchase agreements), and that title in them will pass either on exchange or on completion.

Fittings attract a lot of attention because they do not attract Stamp Duty. It is an offence to artificially increase the cost of the fittings so as to reduce the value of the property so that the purchaser pays less Stamp Duty. Such actions are fraudulent and attract criminal sanctions.

The buyer's solicitor carries out most of the work. Your role and that of your solicitor will be to answer the queries raised as fully and as honestly as possible. You will recall that there is no binding contract to sell or buy land until the contracts have been signed – as immoral as it sounds, both parties can drop out of the transaction at any moment until this point and suffer limited financial consequences.

When you make your calculations of what sums you expect to receive at the end of the transaction, you need to take into account:

- The redemption of any existing mortgage.

- Early mortgage redemption charges.

- Solicitors and other professional fees.

- Any Capital Gains Tax liabilities.

Tax considerations

A sale of a property may well attract tax in the form of Capital Gains Tax. This applies in cases where you have built a new home and have decided to sell it on without living in it and making it your sole and principal home. Capital Gains Tax is imposed on the gains that a party makes on chargeable assets during a tax year. There are various exemptions – such as the disposal of an asset between husband and wife or the sale of a person's principal place of residence. If you think you may have tax liabilities, you would be well advised to contact an accountant.

If you have been running a business from the property (such as a bed and breakfast), there are additional VAT considerations to take into account, particularly if you have been carrying out renovations and have elected to reclaim any VAT spent. In such scenarios consult a tax specialist.

Case Study

This Case Study is based on a true story that was reported in the national press in 2003.

Mr and Mrs Lancaster were in the process of selling their home to Mr and Mrs Spitfire. The Lancaster's received a form requesting particulars about their home from the Spitfire's lawyers.

The form asked the question whether they were aware of "any disputes about this or any neighbouring property" and "whether they had received complaints about anything that they have or have not done as owners". The Lancaster's replied in the negative to both queries.

The transaction completed and the Spitfires bought the house. Some months later the Spitfires ordered some food to be delivered. Unfortunately, their neighbour Mrs Harvard was unhappy about this delivery. Mrs Harvard owned the stretch of land that was the private access road that led up to the Spitfire's home.

It was then that the acidic nature of the relationships in the neighbourhood became apparent. Disputes in relation to the access road had been going on for some years, long before the Spitfires had purchased the property.

The Spitfires claimed against the Lancaster's for failing to disclose this fact. The Lancaster's weakly argued that at the actual time of sale there were no disputes. The judge was not impressed with this argument.

In a court settlement the Lancaster's paid the Spitfires in the region of £70,000 as compensation. The moral: an untruthful or even mistaken disclosure when selling your property can land you in hot water.

CHAPTER 15

Landlord and Tenant Relationships

Many self-build projects result in a part of the development or extension being let out to a tenant. You may be renting out an outhouse, the house itself or the extension to the house. Each of these scenarios brings about a different relationship between you as the landlord and the tenant.

The first option is to have a licence of occupation rather than establishing a tenancy. The advantage to the landlord in establishing a licence is that the tenant (referred to as a licensee) has fewer rights.

The vast majority of lettings are an assured tenancy, more specifically an assured short-hold tenancy. For a tenancy to exist the tenant(s) must:

● be an individual and

● occupy the premises as the principal home.

You also need to ensure that the tenancy is not excluded by any legislation (principally the Housing Act 1988).

Resident landlord

If you are renting out part of your home that you continue to live in, you may be considered a resident landlord. If you are a resident landlord the tenancy may not be assured. This is to prevent certain rights being granted to the tenant due to the complexities of the landlord and the tenant living in such close proximity.

In order for a letting to be considered

as being let as a resident landlord, there are certain criteria that need to be fulfilled; these are to ensure that the:

● Dwelling that is being let forms a part of the building.

● Dwelling is not part of a purpose-built block of flats (ie self-contained flats; this is not the same as a house that has been converted).

● Tenancy was granted by you, the landlord, as an individual (rather than as a company), and you continue to reside in the building.

If you move out during the tenancy the tenant is an assured tenant, together with the protection from eviction that comes with being an assured tenant. However, there are varying degrees of absence that may still ensure that the resident landlord exception applies. If you are no longer a resident landlord and the tenancy was entered into after 28 February 1997, the tenant is an assured shorthold tenant. Older assured tenancies that precede this date are outside the scope of this book.

An assured shorthold will generally last for six months. Where you have an assured shorthold tenancy the landlord is compelled to give the tenant details of the letting, such as:

● The commencement date of the tenancy.

- The rent payable and dates upon which it is to be paid.

- The length of the tenancy.

- The rent review dates.

Most of this information is presented in the assured shorthold tenancy agreement that is widely available from most bookshops. Failure to provide this information is a criminal offence.

At the end of the term the tenant continues to be a statutory periodic tenant, and the landlord will need to give two months notice for any possession.

Responsibility for repairs

A common area of conflict between landlords and tenants is when allocating responsibility for repairs to the rented accommodation. This is further complicated when a tenant withholds paying rent until a repair is rectified. The first step is to establish what a repair is. Generally, the maintenance of and improvements to the premises are not repairs. Nor is a state of disrepair caused by faulty workmanship; however, the line of what constitutes a repair and what is repair to the fabric of the building as a consequence of a design defect is a grey one. If the premises are in a state of disrepair, you need to consider your obligations to keep the premises in a habitable state.

The responsibility for repairs is likely to be set out in the tenancy agreement. If the agreement is silent on this point (or if there is no written agreement), where the premises is furnished it is implied that the landlord warrants that the premises are fit for habitation at the time of the tenancy. If there are common parts to the premises, it is implied that the landlord shall maintain these.

Other terms that are implied for short leases (less than seven years) are for the landlord to:

- Repair the structure and exterior of premises, drains, gutters and external pipes.

- Keep and maintain the appliances (gas, water, electricity, heating etc.).

A landlord has an obligation under the Defective Premises Act 1972 to take reasonable steps to ensure that all persons who may be affected by a defect are kept safe from it; and to ensure that their property is reasonably safe from any damage that may be caused by the defect. The responsibility arises from defects that the landlord knew or ought to know about. This is greater than you may think. A landlord has an implied right to enter the premises, therefore it is deemed that he has a higher standard of knowledge in that he ought to have known about the defect.

If you, the landlord, are also the contractor who built the premises that the tenant is renting, you owe the tenant a duty of care for any negligent work, especially if the work is dangerous, unsafe or defective.

In Chapter 4 (see pages 53–57), we discussed statutory nuisances. Examples of statutory nuisances extend to the state of repair of the premises – for example, it is an offence to: *(text continues on page 137)*

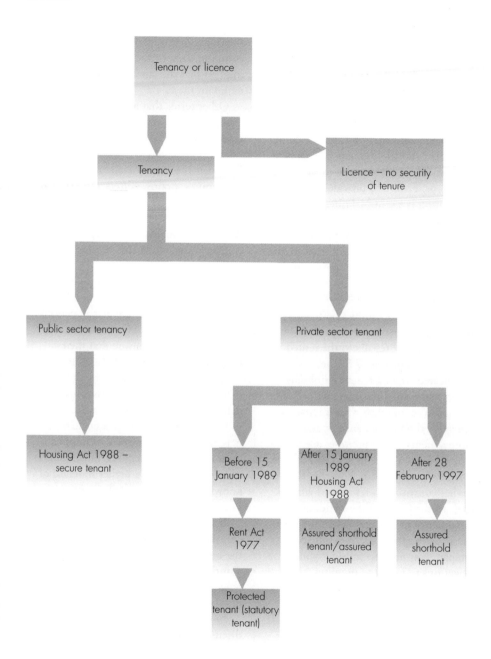

Tenancy or licence.

● Maintain a property that is prejudicial to health or a nuisance.

● Keep a property that emits smoke, noise, fumes, or gases that are prejudicial to health.

● Keep animals that are prejudicial to health.

If the nuisance is prejudicial to health or likely to be prejudicial to health, the local authority may issue an abatement notice. The effect of an abatement notice is discussed in detail in Chapter 4.

If a house is unfit for human habitation, the local authority have additional powers (under the Housing Act 1985) to issue a variety of notices, such as a repair notice, a closing notice – meaning that the premises cannot be used for occupation and a demolition order. In order not to fall foul of the Housing Act 1985, the landlord needs to ensure that the premises:

● Are structurally stable.

● Are free from serious disrepair.

● Are free from any dampness that is prejudicial to the health of the occupants.

● Have adequate heating, lighting and ventilation.

● Have suitable washing facilities (bath, basin, shower etc.).

● Have effective draining of foul water, waste and surface water.

There are other safety obligations that you must deal with:

● An annual CORGI check on the gas appliances carried out by a CORGI-registered engineer.

● All furnishings and fittings to comply with flammability safety standards.

Possession

If the tenant does not leave the premises voluntarily at the end of the term of the assured shorthold tenancy, the landlord needs to go to court to obtain possession. This procedure cannot take place during the first six months of the tenancy. Before going to court for a possession order, the landlord must give the tenant 21 days notice of eviction, at least two months before the date when he requires possession.

The grounds to obtain a court order for possession for an assured shorthold tenancy during the term of the tenancy can either be a mandatory ground or a discretionary ground for possession; the rules governing the procedure and grounds for possession are very complex, and if you are going to seek possession, you must take independent professional advice.

As a general overview, the mandatory grounds for obtaining possession could be:

● The landlord used the dwelling as his sole and principal home and relayed this to the tenant before the commencement of the tenancy.

● The landlord requires the dwelling as

his or his spouse's principal home.

● The mortgage lender is exercising its power of sale.

● The tenancy is for less than eight months and the premises are used as out-of-season holiday accommodation. In this instance the landlord must pass this fact onto the tenant before the commencement of the term and the premises should also have been occupied as a holiday home in the past 12 months, ending with the beginning of the tenancy.

● The landlord intends to reconstruct the whole or a substantial part of the premises.

● Substantial rent arrears, for example:
  ✎ if the rent is payable weekly or fortnightly and eight weeks remain unpaid.
  ✎ if the rent is payable monthly and two months are unpaid.
  ✎ if the rent is payable quarterly and one quarter is unpaid.

The courts have discretionary grounds within which to make a possession order – examples include:

● Alternative accommodation is made available to the tenant on possession.

● Some rent is in arrears (the rent need not be in arrears at the date of the possession hearing).

● Persistent delay in paying the rent.

● Breach of the tenancy agreement. The condition of the dwelling has deteriorated due to waste and neglect.

● The tenant is being or is causing a nuisance.

● There have been incidences of domestic violence.

● Damage to furniture.

● A false statement was made by the tenant in order to induce the landlord to enter into the tenancy.

Protection from eviction

A tenant is afforded extensive protection from harassment and eviction from the landlord. You should be aware that it is a criminal offence to unlawfully evict a tenant from a premises unless you reasonably believe that they no longer live there.

There are some exceptions to the protection afforded to tenants, for example:

● Residential tenant licensors who share the principle home of the landlord licensor or a member of his family.

● The tenancy was granted for non-financial reasons.

As with contracts for the sale of goods and supply of services, there are certain terms that are implied into tenancy agreements, the key one being an implied right for the tenant to have a right of quiet enjoyment of the premises.

Case Study

Mr Blue was an assured shorthold tenant of Mr Red. Mr Red wanted to evict Mr Blue from the premises. Mr Red had a short temper, and whilst he had legitimate grounds for bringing the tenancy to an end, he thought that by pressuring Mr Blue he could evict him quicker and more cheaply than having to go to court to obtain a court order.

Mr Red was mistaken. Mr Red changed the locks and moved Mr Blue's belongings into the corridor. This act of unlawful eviction is an offence. It is unlawful to evict a tenant without a court order if you reasonably believe them to be living in the premises.

If Mr Blue was in the premises at the time and violence was used or was threatened, then criminal sanctions can be levelled at Mr Red. Blue could also take civil proceedings against Mr Red. He could go to court and get an injunction reinstating him or preventing the eviction, and he could also seek damages from Mr Red. The damages that Mr Red could obtain may be substantial as they could be assessed on the difference in value between an empty unit and having a sitting tenant occupying it. There may even be aggravated and exemplary damages on top.

It is no use Mr Red thinking that Mr Blue is a student and will never be able to sue him as Mr Blue may be entitled to legal aid.

KEY POINTS

- Most tenants have an assured shorthold tenancy for a minimum of six months.

- Special rules are in place for landlords who also occupy the premises that are being let.

- Consider any additional income tax liabilities.

CHAPTER 16

Misrepresentations

The word "misrepresentation" is banded about in everyday life with very few people understanding its true meaning in law. Clearly there must be some recompense to a person who suffered a loss because someone bent the truth a little, or was economical with it. We see this every day – people representing certain facts to induce people to enter into a contract, or professionals simply giving wrong advice to their client. All of these are false representations of the facts – a misrepresentation – and the law provides remedies for this, both in established legislation and in case law. This area of law is complex, and professional advice should be sought. However, the aim of this chapter is to make you aware of the scenarios where a misrepresentation has occurred and your remedies as a consequence.

Misrepresentation of a contractual term

It happens all the time, the banter that goes on to induce people to enter into contracts. From the advertising hoarding to the sale floor, and finally in the description of the product – all manner of representations are made: the drill that is faster, more powerful, with a long battery life and extraordinarily strong drill bits – some products even offer you wealth and happiness beyond your wildest dreams.

What we look at here are two types of misrepresentation. The first is a misrepresentation of an actual term of the contract itself, and the other is a misrepresentation that induces you to enter into the contract.

If a party has made a misrepresentation which becomes a term of the contract and the term turns out to be false and you have suffered some form of loss, you are able to claim for damages for a breach of contract.

A misrepresentation of fact that you rely upon and induces you to enter into a contract will also entitle you to claim for a breach of contract. Most level-headed people are able to realise when a sales pitch is a mere puff and to be taken with a pinch of salt. However, difficulties arise when deciding what a sales puff is, and what is expected from the product or contract.

The Misrepresentation Act 1967 sets out the law in relation to misrepresentations that affect the terms of contracts and contractual relations. There are three main parts to this act. The first is where during contractual negotiations a statement is made that is proved to be false. In the case of the person making the statement, it is a defence if he can show that he had reasonable grounds for proving that the facts represented were true. This section also makes a contractual term that attempts to exclude liability for negligent misstatements ineffective unless the party that is trying to exclude the clause can show that it is fair and reasonable to exclude such a liability.

If a misrepresentation has been made and you enter into the contract and the

Case Study

Richard was after the latest drill for his self-build project. As he was using a variety of materials for his project, he knew that an ordinary drill would not suffice, but his budget was tight. He scoured the magazines until he found the drill that he felt suited his budget. The Maxdrill came with a variety of drill bits proven to drill through inch-thick metal. Richard went to his hardware store and spoke to the salesman, who told him that the drill bits were "indestructible".

Richard parted with his money and began work with the drill. Several drills later the drill bits began to fall apart and the drill itself began to need recharging every hour or so. Richard was at his wits' end.

There are two issues here. The first is the claim under the Sale of Goods and Supply of Service Acts; the second is for the false statement made by the salesperson to Richard that induced Richard to enter into the contract.

If the salesman honestly believed in the statement that he made, Richard would be struggling to prove a misrepresentation. However, the salesman knew that several people had returned the Maxdrill with similar complaints.

When Richard discussed this with the salesman, he was told by the salesman that if he bothered to research the Maxdrill on the Internet or in the building literature he would have known that it was not suitable for his needs. It is no defence for the salesperson to suggest that if Richard had bothered to check and uncover the facts for himself that he would have unmasked the misrepresentation. Conversely, if Richard had checked and did know the salesperson was misrepresenting the facts, he would not have a case for misrepresentation.

The salesperson was employed by the DIY store, therefore Richard had a claim for breach of contract (not to mention the other grounds under the Sale of Goods Act, and possibly the Consumer Protection Act) against the DIY store.

---

misrepresentation becomes a term of the contract, you, as the affected party, have a right to rescind (treat the contract as though it is at an end) the contract.

The second limb of the Misrepresentation Act is to entitle the affected party to damages as a consequence of the misrepresentations. If a representation upon which you rely induces you to enter into a contract, you are entitled to damages for the misrepresentation. For example, if a surveyor warranted that the defective house you are purchasing was worth X but in fact was worth Y, the damages that you may be entitled to (if you can prove a misrepresentation) would be the difference between the defective property's market value at the time of the survey and the price paid.

Unless the statement was made fraudulently, you would not be entitled to any recompense if the person that made the statement can show that they had reasonable grounds for making the statement. It is possible to rescind the contract for false statements that are relied upon to enter into the contract, but this remedy is at the court's discretion. Trying to prove fraudulent misrep-resentation requires a high burden of proof and is outside the scope of this book.

Negligent statements

This area of misrepresentation moves away from contract law and more into the law of tort, which covers normal human relations; you do not need a contract to bring an action in tort. One of the distinctions between a claim under tort and one under contract is the level of damages you can claim.

For a breach of contract, your claim would be to put you in the position had

Case Study

Digdeep Contractors were about to enter into a contract with Mr Scatty, who had prepared all the tender documents himself. In these he stated that the ground and soil conditions were suitable for the construction of the house. Digdeep Contractors took him at his word and based their tender price and programme on this and the other statements made in the tender documents. The building contract (of which the tender documents formed a part) that was entered into did not place any obligations on the contractor to investigate or consider the ground conditions.

Once the works started it was clear that the soil was not suitable for the project at hand. Digdeep were upset about this, as their quote and programme had to be reconsidered. Mr Scatty might have to pay them damages as a consequence. However, Mr Scatty had inserted a provision in the contract that excluded all liability for statements and misrepresentations made in the tender documents.

Whether this exclusion could be relied upon by Mr Scatty would depend on whether in the circumstances it would be considered fair and reasonable to be included having regard to the circumstances of the parties – or ought reasonably to have been in the contemplation of the parties at the time that the contract was made.

the contract been properly performed. In tort, your claim for damages would be to put you in the position had the tort never been committed. In many scenarios you will find that there is an overlap between the two, and you have to consider which is more favourable. For example, if you instruct a surveyor and he makes a misrepresentation, this is both a breach of contract and a negligent statement (tort).

A case for negligent misstatement normally arises where a special relationship exists between a professional and a client – for example, between a surveyor or architect and his client.

A duty does not arise between a professional and the world at large.

There has to be a special relationship, a certain amount of proximity. Such a relationship would need to show that the person affected by the negligent misstatement relied upon the statement to his detriment and that the person making it knew that such reliance would be placed upon this statement.

This proximity has been pushed in recent years, and would even establish a liability for any statements made by a surveyor who is instructed by a mortgage lender to survey a house for the purposes of a loan. However, this responsibility would not extend to subsequent owners of the premises.

In order to establish a case against a party making (text continues on page 144)

Case Study

Mr Blair bought a plot of land on the basis of his professional adviser telling him that planning consent had been obtained to build a house on the plot. Unfortunately this was not the case and no planning consent had been obtained. Mr Blair's professional adviser had made a negligent statement. The plot cost £40,000, and the value of the plot without consent was just over half that at £25,000. With a completed house, the plot would be worth £50,000.

In contract law, Mr Blair would be entitled to be placed in the position had the representation been true. This means that he would be entitled

to £25,000 (the projected value of the plot and house being £50,000 less the actual value of the plot without planning consent: £25,000).

In tort, Mr Blair would be entitled to the damages that would put him in the position had the misrepresentation never been made. Therefore he is entitled to the cost of the plot (£40,000) less the actual value of the plot without consent (£25,000). This means that he is only entitled to £15,000 in damages.

Conversely, there are scenarios where it makes financial sense to bring the claim under tort rather than for breach of contract.

a negligent misstatement, you need to show that:

● A special relationship existed between the affected person and the party that made the statement;

● It is fair and reasonable for a duty to be owed from the person making the statement to the affected party; and

● The affected party relied on the statement to his detriment.

The context in which the statements are made must also be considered. If they are made in a social situations or as general commentary, it is very unlikely that the professional would be liable for any misrepresentations made. Negligent misstatement is one of the few exceptions where one can claim for pure economic loss arising out of negligence.

SUMMARY

● Most misrepresentations fall under two headings, but there is some overlap: contractual misrepresentation (contract) and negligent statements (tort).

● Contractual misrepresentations are, broadly speaking, incidences where a party is induced into entering into a contract as a consequence of the false representation or the false representation is a term of the contract.

● There is a defence if the party making the false representations (misrepresentation) honestly believed the statement was true.

● One can, depending on the circumstances, claim for damages or rescind the contract.

● Claims for negligent statements are brought under the law of tort and generally cover negligent statements made by professionals to their clients.

● The damages that one can claim for differ depending upon whether the claim is under tort or contract. For a breach of contract, your claim would be to put you in the position had the contract been properly performed. In tort, your claim for damages would be to put you in the position had the tort never been committed.

● Consider that a disclaimer may only be effective if it is fair and reasonable under the circumstances for the disclaimer to apply.

Home Extensions and Renovations

The aim of Part Two is to focus upon the issues that are specific to those readers carrying out extensions to their property. Most of the topics covered in Part One impact upon those carrying out extensions; however, there are certain topics that are considered in greater detail (the sale and purchase of land and planning law), and new topics are introduced.

When carrying out extension works to a home, you are likely to have regard to the interests of a superior landlord. These interests are documented in the lease. As with contracts, there are some general commercial norms; however, each lease is different and must be read to uncover those provisions that are particular to it.

You may also be buying a part of your neighbour's land on which you intend to build your extension. Building extensions introduce the law that governs building work that is adjacent to your neighbour's wall.

As you are aware, for the purposes of planning law building works are likely to be a development requiring planning consent. However, certain works to domestic homes are exempt. We have already covered these in earlier chapters, but there are further exemptions which relate to extensions.

Readers carrying out works of a minor nature are most likely to enter into the JCT Home Builders Form of Building Contract with their contractor. This section examines that particular contract clause by clause.

CHAPTER 17

Additional Planning Considerations for Home Improvements

This chapter builds upon the topics introduced in Chapter 3 (see pages 26–52). By now you are aware of the steps that you need to consider when deciding whether you need to make a planning application. In order to recap, ask yourself if you are carrying out a development. If you are, the general rule is that you need to make a planning application. However, there are certain exclusions to this general rule, which are listed in the planning acts (General Permitted Developments Order). Even if your development falls into one of these exclusions you need to consider additional factors, such as whether an Article 4 directive is in force, the Conservation (Natural Habitats) Regulations 1994 and any further considerations specific to listed buildings and Conservation Areas.

Where the works are to result in the construction of a building which will be used for unlawful purposes, or if the building operations themselves are unlawful, the planning exemptions do not apply.

Additional considerations

The additional general exceptions that are allocated to developments within the curtilage of a dwelling house are set out, in detail, in Schedule 2 of the General Permitted Development Order (GPDO) 1995 – and these are set out, in part, below. The exceptions are listed with reference to classes; each class then has a subheading describing, in detail, the scope of what is permitted. For example,

the following are the general headings for permitted developments (meaning they are developments to domestic dwelling houses which are exempt from requiring a formal planning application). The specific limitations and tolerances for each class are considered later on.

● Class A: enlargement, improvement or other alteration of a dwelling house.

● Class B: enlargement of a dwelling house consisting of an alteration or addition to its roof.

● Class C: any other alteration to the roof of a dwelling house.

● Class D: erection or construction of a porch outside the external door of a dwelling house.

● Class E: provision within the curtilage of a dwelling house of any building or enclosure, swimming pool, or other pool required for a purpose incidental to the enjoyment of the dwelling house.

● Class F: provision within the curtilage of a dwelling house of a hard surface for any purpose incidental to the enjoyment of the dwelling house.

● Class G: provision within the curtilage of a dwelling house of a container for the storage of oil for domestic heating.

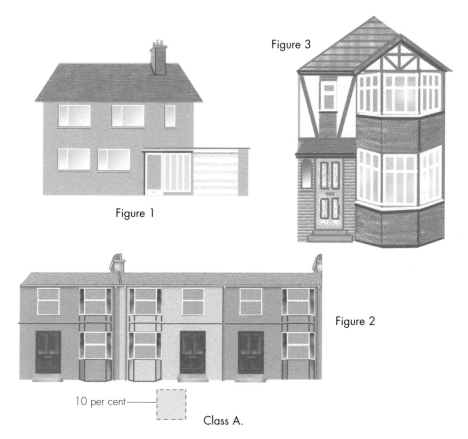

Figure 3

Figure 1

Figure 2

10 per cent

Class A.

● Class H: installation, alteration or replacement of a satellite antenna on a dwelling house or within the curtilage of a dwelling house.

Each class has its own limitations as to the permitted scope of the development:

Class A: any enlargement, improvement or other alteration of a dwelling house is a permitted development, provided:

● It does not increase the cubic content of the original house. (Fig. 1.) In the case of a terraced house by more than 50 cu m or 10 per cent, whichever is greater. (Fig. 2.) In any other case by more than 70 cu m or 15 per cent, whichever is greater. In any event by more than 115 cu m.

● The area being worked upon does not exceed the highest part of the roof of the original dwelling house. (Fig. 3.)

● The area being developed does not encroach onto the highway any more than the part of the original house nearest to the highway or any point 20 m from the highway. (Fig. 4, see page 148.)

147

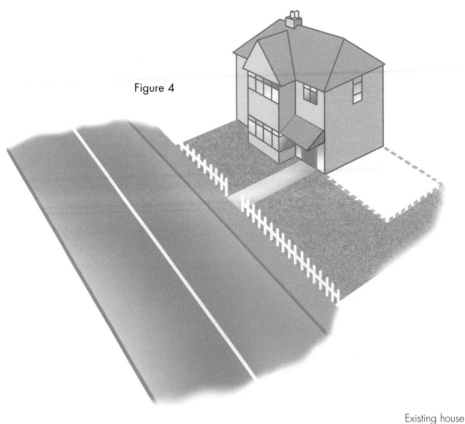

Figure 4

Class A.

● In cases other than the insertion, erection or alteration of a window in an existing wall; the development is within 2 m of the boundary of the existing house and would not exceed 4 m in height. (Fig. 5.)

● The total ground area covered by the buildings within the curtilage (other than the original house) does not exceed 50 per cent of the curtilage (excluding the ground area of the original dwelling house).

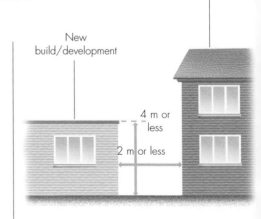

Figure 5

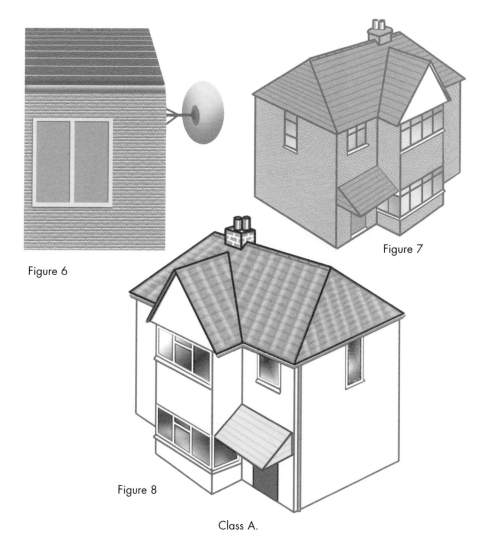

Figure 6

Figure 7

Figure 8

Class A.

- It does not involve the installation, erection, alteration or replacement of a satellite antenna (see class H, page 155). (Fig. 6.)

- It does not consist of or include the erection of a building within the curtilage of a listed building.

- It does not consist of or include the cladding of any part of the exterior with, artificial stone, timber plastic or tiles. (Fig. 7.)

- It does not involve works to the roof. (Fig. 8.)

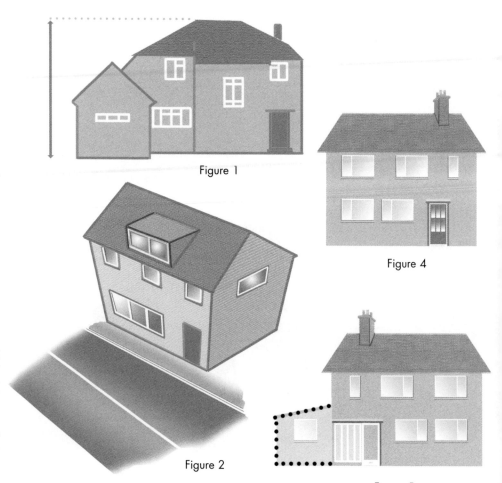

Figure 1

Figure 4

Figure 2

Figure 5

Figure 3

Class B.

Class B: the enlargement of a dwelling house consisting of an alteration or addition to its roof is a permitted development, provided that the works do not:

● Exceed the highest part of the roof of the original dwelling house. (Fig. 1.)

● As a result of the works, any part of the dwelling house would extend beyond the plane of any existing roof slope which fronts a highway. (Fig. 2.)

● Increase the cubic content of the dwelling house by 40 cu m in the case of a terraced house (Fig. 3), or in any other case by 50 cu m.

● (In the case of the resulting building) exceed the cubic content of the original dwelling house by 50 cu m or 10 per cent, whichever is greater (Fig. 4), or in any other case by 70 cu m, or 15 per cent, whichever is greater, and in any event no more than 115 cu m. (Fig. 5.)

● Involve works on land in National Parks, Conservation Areas and Areas of Outstanding National Beauty etc.

Class C: any other alteration to the roof of a dwelling house is a permitted development, provided that the alterations do not materially alter the shape of the dwelling house.

Class D: it is a permitted development to erect or construct a porch outside the external door of a dwelling house, provided that:

● The ground area (measured externally) from the new structure does not exceed 3 sq m.

● Any part of the structure is no more than 3 m above ground level.

● Any part of the structure is within 2 m of any boundary of the existing house with a highway.

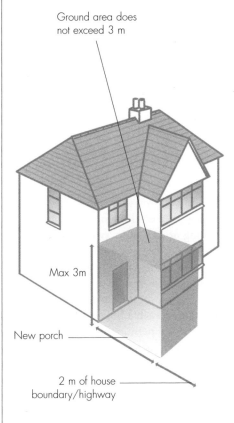

Ground area does not exceed 3 m

Max 3m

New porch

2 m of house boundary/highway

Class D: construction of a porch is permitted.

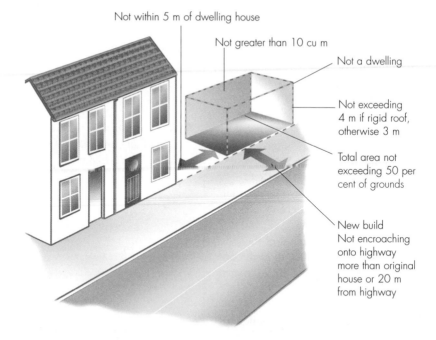

Not within 5 m of dwelling house

Not greater than 10 cu m

Not a dwelling

Not exceeding 4 m if rigid roof, otherwise 3 m

Total area not exceeding 50 per cent of grounds

New build Not encroaching onto highway more than original house or 20 m from highway

Class E: it is permissible to build a new building within the curtilage of a dwelling house.

Class E: the provision within the curtilage of a dwelling house of any building or enclosure, swimming pool, or other pool required for a purpose incidental to the enjoyment of the dwelling house as such, or the maintenance, improvement or other alteration of such a building or enclosure is a permitted development. The restrictions are that:

● The works do not relate to a dwelling or satellite antenna.

● The area being developed does not encroach onto the highway any more than the part of the original house nearest to the highway or any point

20 m from the highway (whichever is nearer to the highway).

● The new building would not have a cubic content greater than 10 cu m and not be within 5 m of the dwelling house.

● The height of the new building or enclosure would not exceed 4 m in the case of a building with a rigid roof or 3 m in any other case.

● The total area covered by the building would not exceed 50 per cent of the total area of the curtilage of the grounds (excluding the ground area of the original dwelling house).

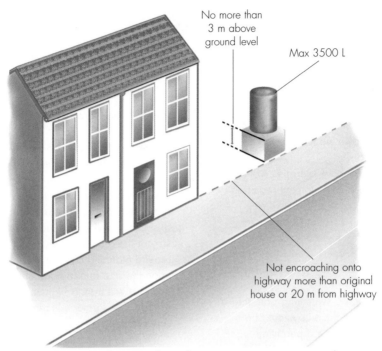

No more than
3 m above
ground level

Max 3500 L

Not encroaching onto
highway more than original
house or 20 m from highway

Class G: development of an oil storage container is permitted.

● In the case of land in National Parks, Conservation Areas and Areas of Outstanding National Beauty etc., or land within the curtilage of a listed building, it would not consist of the provision, alteration or improvement of a building with a cubic content greater than 10 cu m.

Class F: the provision within the curtilage of a dwelling house of a hard surface for any purpose incidental to the enjoyment of the dwelling house is a permitted development – this covers things like paving the driveway.

Class G: the provision within the curtilage of a dwelling house of a container for the storage of oil for domestic heating is a permitted development, provided that:

● The container does not exceed 3500 L.

● Any part of the container would not be more than 3 m above ground level.

● The area being developed does not encroach onto the highway any more than the part of the original house nearest to the highway or any point 20 m from the highway (whichever is nearer to the highway).

Case Study

Darius and Cristina have been living in their house for several years and Darius has decided that he wants to pave his driveway, build a swimming pool and build some skylights into his roof. He also wants to install a big satellite dish.

All the above activities would constitute a development requiring planning consent. The next step is for Darius and Cristina to ascertain whether the Town and Country Planning (General Permitted Development Order) 1995 provides for exemptions.

Building a swimming pool that is incidental to the enjoyment of a dwelling house is a permitted development, therefore it is unlikely that planning consent is required. However, Cristina would like the swimming pool to have a roof and be enclosed so that it can be used during the winter months. If this new building housing the swimming pool is going to:

● Have a cubic content exceeding 10 cu m.

● Exceed 3 m in height; or

● Cover more than 50 per cent of land relative to the area of the house;

they will need to apply for planning consent.

The paving of the driveway, while a development, falls within one of the exceptions and no planning consent is required.The skylights to the roof are an interesting proposition. If the design of the skylights increases the size of the roof, this activity may require planning consent, depending upon the size and also whether the skylights will front a highway or the garden. The former will require separate consent.

Finally, the installation of a satellite antenna does not generally need planning consent. Darius intends to install a satellite greater than 70 cm in diameter, so he falls outside of the exemption and planning consent needs to be applied for.

Once Darius and Cristina have established which activities require consent and which are exempt, they should examine any external factors that may effect the exemptions – for example Article 4 directives, restrictive covenants etc.

Class H: generally, the installation, alteration or replacement of a satellite antenna on a dwelling house or within the curtilage of a dwelling house is a permitted development; however, there are a whole host of restrictions that are applicable to this permitted development. Class H does not permit the installation, alteration or replacement of a satellite antenna if:

● The size of the antenna (excluding the mountings, reinforcing rim etc.) when measured in any dimension does not exceed:

✎ 45 cm in the case of an antenna to be installed on a chimney.

✎ 90 cm in the case of an antenna to be installed other than a chimney.

✎ The highest part of the antenna would not exceed the highest part of the roof or chimney when installed on the roof and chimney respectively.

✎ There is another satellite antenna on another dwelling house in the curtilage of the dwelling house.

✎ In the case of land in National Parks, Conservation Areas and Areas of Outstanding National Beauty etc., if it would consist of the installation of the antenna on the chimney, or a building that exceeds 15 m in height.

KEY POINTS

● The general rule is that most works to a house will amount to a development requiring planning consent.

● There are certain permitted developments that provide for an exception to the general rule.

● These permitted developments have their own limitations that must be adhered to. Developments that exceed the limitation of a "permitted development" will require planning consent.

● Even if the works fall within the scope of a permitted development, you will need to check any external factors that may affect the exemptions – for example, Article 4 directives, restrictive covenants etc.

SUMMARY

Many home improvers and self-builders spend an inordinate amount of time with the planning applications for their development. It may be wisest to pass this risk on to an architect, who would not only prepare the plans and amend them accordingly, but would also take the risks in making the application.

The UK planning laws are unnecessarily convoluted, and are due to be overhauled between 2005–08. However, with the law as it currently stands, there are certain developments that are permitted by the planning acts and so do not require planning consent, provided that the works are carried out within the parameters set out by the planning acts.

CHAPTER 18

Party Walls

A common issue that arises when building an extension to an existing property is the effect that your work will have on neighbouring properties. This is especially true in city housing, where many houses are effectively built within metres of each other or are semi-detached or even terraced.

If you are building alongside or on your neighbour's wall or excavating within 3 m or 6 m of it, you need to consider a rather obscure but important Act of Parliament – the Party Wall Etc. Act 1996 (applicable only to works in England and Wales). This act sets out the steps you need to take to inform your neighbour of your proposed works, and how to go about agreeing the scope and any possible additional works that may be required to support (or underpin) your neighbour's wall.

If you don't abide by the provisions of the act, you could find yourself on the receiving end of a civil law suit or a court order forcing you to remove your work. The good news is that with a little communication with your affected neighbours, and providing them with the appropriate information in good time, the works should proceed without a hitch.

The aim of this chapter is to give you a working knowledge of the act. The act does not change the ownership of the walls, nor does it deal with boundary disputes.

Does the act apply to your project?

First, establish the boundary line indicating ownership of the affected properties by examining plans of your land/property from the Land Registry (www.landreg.gov.uk).

Now consider these three general circumstances where the act is most likely to apply:

- Carrying out works to an existing party wall or structure: if the existing wall strides both your and your neighbour's property, and you are carrying out works to the shared wall. (Minor works, such as putting up shelving, minor drilling or installing electrical sockets – carried out on your half of the wall – are likely to fall outside the act.)

- Where the new wall will be built at or astride the boundary line, for example if the wall is to be built hard up to your neighbour's wall. This may seem unfair, but you are likely to have footings and foundations that will project onto your neighbour's land.

- If the proposed wall is wholly on your land and you are excavating within 3 m or 6 m (depending upon the proposed depth of the excavations) from your neighbour's wall.

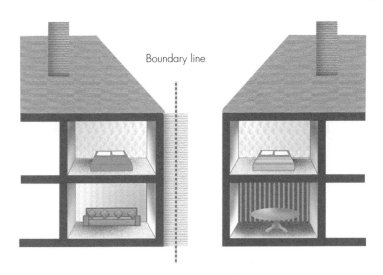

Party wall of an existing building.

What is a party wall?

The act sets out in detail what a party wall is. Most readers will be able to exercise their common sense when trying to ascertain if the wall is a party wall or not. For example, a party wall is a wall that is either part of an existing building, separates two or more buildings or is merely a party wall fence. If you read the act or books that discuss the act in detail, you will also come across references to party structures. These are the vertical divisions in properties.

Examples of the type of works that are

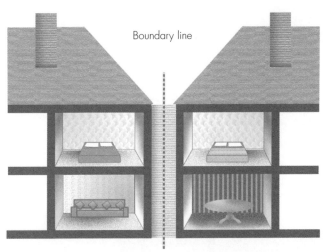

Party wall separating two buildings.

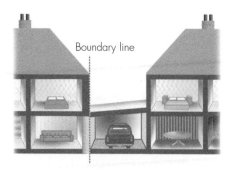

Boundary line

Vertical divisions.

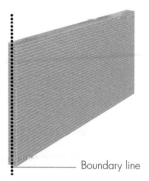

Boundary line

Party wall fence.

typically carried out by home improvers to party walls are:

● Inserting damp-proofing.

● Raising the height of a wall or increasing its thickness.

● Using the wall for loadbearing reasons.

Each one of these activities (in addition to the three key ones listed left) requires you to serve a notice on your adjoining owner and consider the provisions of the act.

If you are carrying out one of the three types of work to a party wall, you need serve a notice on all your affected neighbours. This sounds incredibly formal, but it is not – your neighbour, for

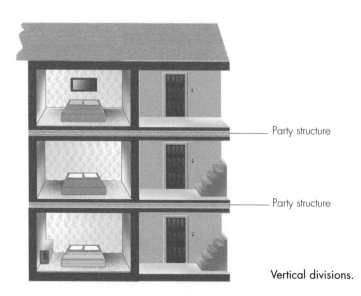

Party structure

Party structure

Vertical divisions.

the purposes of the act, means any person who has an interest greater than a yearly tenancy in the adjoining property. Clearly, if there is more than one adjoining owner, you will need to serve a notice on each of the affected parties. The notice need not take any particular format, but it must be in writing. The details that the notice must contain differ depending upon the nature of the works to the party wall.

If you are doing works upon a shared wall that strides both your property and your neighbour's, the notice must:

● Be given to your neighbour at least two months before you propose to start the works.

● State your name and address.

● Describe the works (give your neighbour as much information as possible, e.g. provide plans, sections, consents and any load requirements that may apply).

● State the proposed start date of the works.

If you are building a wall up to or astride the boundary line, the notice must contain the same details set out above. However, the notice need only be served one month before the planned start date.

Where you are excavating 3 m or 6 m (depending upon the depth of your excavations) from your neighbour's property, your notice must be served one month before the proposed start date. It must also include the following additional details:

● An outline of your proposed works.

● An indication as to whether you propose to strengthen or underpin your neighbour's wall.

● Full plans showing the proposed site and depth of the excavations.

The rules governing excavations in the vicinity of a party wall need to be considered more carefully.

If you are excavating within 3 m of your adjoining neighbour's building or structure and those excavations go deeper than the deepest part of your neighbour's foundations, then you need to serve a notice.

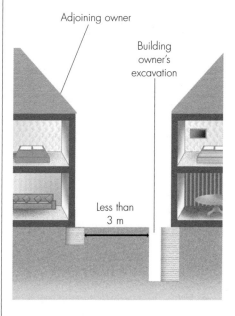

Within 3 m of an adjoining building.

159

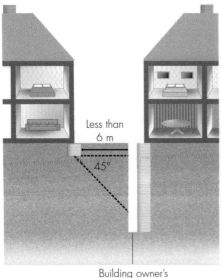

Less than
6 m

45°

Building owner's
excavation

Within 6 m of an adjoining building.

The 6 m rule comes into affect when you are excavating within 6 m of your neighbour's building or wall and where your works pierce an imaginary line drawn at 45 degrees from the bottom of your neighbour's wall or structure.

This is why, for the notice governing excavations 3 m or 6 m from your

neighbour's wall or structure, you must clearly state whether you intend on under-pinning, strengthening etc. the wall, in addition to the full plans showing the extent of the excavations and position of the proposed new building.

Effect of giving the notice

Once you have issued the correct notice (depending upon the type of work that you are carrying out), you must await confirmation from your neighbour(s) that they consent to the works.

This piece of legislation has a very annoying provision in it – if you have not received your neighbour's written consent within 14 days of serving the notice, a dispute is deemed to have arisen between you! However, if you consult your affected neighbours and take into account their concerns at the earliest stages (at least once you have a concrete idea of your proposals), this scenario should never arise.

Your neighbour(s) may give you a counter-notice within 14 days of your notice, setting out any modifications or additional work that they would want carried out.

KEY POINTS

- If you are carrying out significant works on or adjacent to a boundary wall or excavating within 3 m or 6 m of it, you need to consider the provisions of the Party Walls Etc. Act.

- The act provides for a notice to be issued upon your neighbours.

- If you are unable to agree the scope of works or payment of it, you can appoint one or two surveyors who will reach an award, which sets out the responsibilities of each party and the proportion of the payments from each neighbour for the works.

A "dispute" does not mean that a trip to court is in order. The act provides for a simple approach to dispute resolution. The parties should try to agree to appoint a single surveyor who acts as an adjudicator. If you cannot agree upon one, each party appoints their own surveyor; these two surveyors then appoint a third surveyor. The dispute is settled by a decision from the surveyor(s). You may decide that you do not need a surveyor, in which case you may try to agree the dispute between yourselves. If you do decide upon this route, remember that all agreements must be in writing and signed by all the parties.

If you have appointed a surveyor or surveyors, they will prepare an "award", a document that sets out who needs to do what work and when. It also provides for the surveyor(s) to have access to the works to ensure that the works are being carried out in accordance with the award. The role of the surveyors is to reach an award in a fair and impartial manner.

The award (or your agreement with your neighbour) also sets out which party is responsible to pay for the works. The general rule is that the party that initiated and wishes to progress with the works is the party that pays for them. However, if the wall is a neighbouring wall that has fallen into disrepair, or the neighbouring owner wishes the additional work to be carried out solely for his benefit, then the costs for the works will be proportioned accordingly.

The practical impact of works to party walls inevitably results in access having to be granted, and may even mean that workman may have to access your neighbour's premises. Your neighbour will have to grant access to your workman, and conversely, you must give your neighbour at least 14 days prior notice. It is unlikely that your neighbour will restrict entry, as to do so is an offence that is prosecuted in a magistrates' court.

The rights of your neighbour allow him to appoint a second surveyor. He is also entitled:

● Not to suffer any unnecessary inconvenience.

● To be compensated for any damages.

● To request an advance security payment to protect his position if works are stopped before being completed (these monies can be held by solicitors).

The surveyor's award is both final and binding unless and until it is amended by the courts. Each owner has 14 days within which to appeal the award to the court. If you are going to appeal, you need to show that you believe that the surveyor or surveyor's decision is fundamentally wrong.

Additional considerations

The notices only last for 12 months, so assuming you get consent you must start work within 12 months.

The act does not resolve a boundary dispute, nor does it necessarily change the ownership of the wall. You must also ensure that your works conform to the appropriate building and planning regulations.

CHAPTER 19

The JCT Building Contract for Home Builders

If you are carrying out works of a simple nature, such as an extension or kitchen fit-out, the most likely contract that you are going to use is the JCT Home Builders contract. The JCT produce two versions of this contract: one is just the building contract, and the other, newer version is specifically designed for home builders (in England and Wales) employing both consultants and a contractor to complete a project. The contract, which comes with two forms of appointment, costs about £15 at time of writing.

Who are you going to employ?

Before employing a contractor to undertake building work, you should consider who is going to prepare the drawings for the contractor to work from. For example, if you are only employing a contractor to carry out specialist works (such as the piling), he is likely to prepare his own designs. In this scenario you only need a single contract between yourself and the contractor. If these works are fairly simple, the type of contract to use is the (original) JCT Building Contract for Homeowners/Occupiers 1999, where no consultant is employed.

However, if your works are more likely to involve extensive internal refurbishment or a complete new build, in all likelihood you are probably going to employ various consultants (such as an architect, structural engineer and quantity surveyor) to prepare the drawings, obtain planning consent and cost the project etc.

The JCT Form of Contract for Homeowners/Occupiers 2001 is designed for projects where you, the employer, employ both consultants and a contractor. In legal terms, what you have is separate contracts between yourself and the contractor, architect and structural engineer (or other consultants). Therefore, if the building is not built in accordance with the architect's designs, you are able to sue the contractor. Conversely, if the contractor built the building in accordance with the design but the design is faulty, then your claim is against the architect.

Clearly, in the event of things going wrong it can get messy when allocating blame – it is usually preferable to have one party responsible for the entire works. Unfortunately, the UK industry is geared so that if you want snazzy designs you are likely to have to employ a separate architect and contractor.

The JCT Homeowners/Occupiers Contract with Consultant's Appointments 2001

In the pack are two forms of consultant appointments, a building contract and guidance notes. The contract and appointments are devoid of legal jargon and are both Crystal Marked for their clarity in the use of English. The JCT advises that the contracts are to be used for home improvements, repairs and extensions.

The Building Contract

On page 1 insert the names of the parties you are contracting with. Yours will be easy, but remember the general rule is that it is the party named in the contract who will have the right to sue.

Check what entity the contractor is proposing to enter into the contract as. If it is a company, do a quick check at Companies House. If the contractor is a partnership, make sure that all partners enter into the contract and sign it together with witnesses.

Finally, on this page the contract asks you to set out which consultants you propose to employ. This is really for the clarification of everyone's role and to assist the team that you have employed to co-ordinate their efforts.

Page 2 [B] has a minor provision which could cause an unexpected delay: it provides that the contractor will not start the works until all planning/party wall etc. consents have been obtained. This is likely to be the responsibility of the architect.

On page 3 you need to consider when to pay the contractor and how much. Do you want to give him an incentive and pay him a given amount once he achieves certain milestones, or just pay him the whole lot at the end?

The contract also allows you to withhold five per cent of the total sum for three months. Depending upon the nature of the contractor's work, you may wish to lengthen this period – anything up to one year is reasonable.

I suggest handwriting an additional number 3 to [F] along the lines that if the contractor does not finish the works by the completion date or within the period specified, he shall pay you (the employer) a daily rate until the works are complete. (This is a liquidated damages clause.) Remember, any manuscript amendments will need to be initialled by both parties to the contract in order to be enforceable.

Under "[H] Insurance", ensure that the contractor provides you with up-to-date evidence of his insurance cover and that the cover is sufficient for any losses that you may suffer.

On the last page, "[I] Working hours" sets out the dates and times that the contractor may work. These working hours must mirror the conditions set by your local authority. Planning conditions often set out the hours of permitted work, typically 8.30 am to 5 pm Monday to Saturday, with no work on a Sunday. However, these times will vary with each authority.

In the signature box check that two of the contractor's directors correctly sign on behalf of the company, or in the case of a partnership that all the partners sign, and that their signatures have been witnessed.

Consultant's appointments

On page 1 insert the names of the parties that you are contracting with. If the consultant is a company, don't forget to do the basic checks.

Page 1 lists the services of the consultant. Check these very carefully to ensure that everything you want the consultant to do is covered. If it is not listed here, and you ask the consultant to carry out an additional task, you will have to pay him extra.

Each governing body produces a

comprehensive list of services for that professional – for example, contact the RIBA (Royal Institute of British Architects) for architects' services or the ACE (Association of Consulting Engineers) for engineering services.

On page 5[B], there is a short list of exclusions to the services. One of these is party walls. There is no reason why you cannot expressly include this as a service and cross out this exclusion. However, make sure the consultant is a qualified party wall surveyor, and be aware that the consultant is likely to price for this. Party wall awards can delay the works and increase costs if disputed.

As with the contractor, request evidence of the consultant's insurance [C].

In the section headed "Conditions" there is a copyright provision in part 2. This is very useful and should not be deleted or amended by the consultant (for example, to be made subject to you paying him his fees). The clause retains the copyright of the drawings with the consultant. However, the consultant gives you – as the employer – a licence to use these drawings for any additional development incidental to the project for which the drawings were prepared.

KEY POINTS

● The Home Builders Contract may not necessarily be the best for your particular project – if in doubt, consult a professional.

● Read the contract and the guidance notes.

● Do not be pressured into signing the contractor's or the consultant's standard terms of appointment. The JCT contract is an industry standard form of building contract.

Appendix I

Scottish Law

A solicitor admitted in England and Wales does not practice Scottish law, which is regarded as a foreign jurisdiction. This book is written from the perspective of the law of England and Wales. However, there is a significant overlap between the two jurisdictions and numerous similarities. The Scots have a proud and distinct difference in their heritage, education, culture and laws to that of England. Even the actual roots of Scottish Law differ to those of English law, which (along with Welsh law and that of Northern Ireland) is based on case law decided by judges and kings over hundreds of years; these cases were then codified in parliamentary legislation, together with other forms of legislation put forward by parliament. Scotland's legal roots are more akin to the rest of Europe. Its laws are based on old Roman law, with a bit of Germanic law thrown in. Finally, Scotland has its own parliament that generates its own laws. Having said all that, the UK Parliament is supreme over the Scottish Parliament (and the UK Parliament is in turn superseded by the European Parliament).

There are many similarities between the two legal systems, and as this book is intended to be an overview of the legal topics covered, many of the issues and topics will be similar on a general level, but different in detail.

For example, for a contract to be valid in English law there needs to be an offer, an acceptance of that offer and consideration (benefit). Scottish contract law does not require consideration (benefit) in order for the contract to be valid. This means that in Scotland it is valid to have a contract that can compel a person to carry out a task for another person and not receive any benefit for carrying out this task. Scottish law does permit for a third party, that is not a party to the contract, to benefit from the contractual provisions – the Scots just happened to consider this concept hundreds of years before the English!

Scottish property law is directly descendent from Roman law. There are some interesting and subtle differences. In Scotland you cannot generally separate the ownership of the land and the property; the two are fused as one, although there are exceptions to this rule.

KEY POINTS

● This book is intended as an overview of the laws of England and Wales.

● While the concepts of English and Scottish law are sometimes very similar, the details are different – consult a legal advisor who specialises in Scottish law.

Appendix II

Latin Terms

Many solicitors and court procedures still use Latin terms. There is a drive to remove all Latin terms from the legal system, and this change is adopted by many. However, this short guide should help you in relation to the most common Latin terms that you may come across. Do not use Latin phrases – it will be frowned upon.

LATIN	ENGLISH
Abundas cautela non nocet	An abundance of caution does one no harm.
Actus reus	Guilty act.
Audi alteram partem	Listen to the other side – essentially this means that there are two sides to an argument.
Caveat emptor	Buyer beware – the risks associated with the transaction rest with the buyer – or his solicitor!
Codicil	Amending a will.
Contra proferentum	An onerous term in a contract is to be constructed against the person relying upon it – for example, an ambiguous liability clause will be construed by the courts against the person relying on it to exclude or limit their liability.
De minimis	Minimal – in law the courts will ignore matters of a minor or inconsequential nature.
Ex turpi causa non oritur actio	No right of action can arise from an immoral act or illegal contract.
Fiat justitia ruat coelum	This literally means 'let justice be done or the heavens fall'. Essentially, this phrase highlights the overriding principle that justice must be done.
Ignorantia juris neminem excusat	Ignorance of the law is no excuse (defence).
Mea culpa	I am to blame.
Quantum meruit	The amount that is worth – a reasonable amount. This is common in contracts where the sum of money is not specified. The contractor is entitled to monies on a *quantum meruit* basis, i.e. a reasonable sum of money for the works carried out.
Restitutio in integrum	Restoration of the parties to the position that they were in before the contract was entered into. This scenario arises where a contract is rescinded.
Volenti non fit injuria	No injury is done to one that consents.

Glossary

Abatement A pro-rata reduction of a debt or claim against monies owed. It is unclear whether a withholding notice is required where a party intends to abate monies owed to a contractor. Prudent employers would be advised to issue a withholding notice to a Contractor to prevent any potential disputes.

Abode Place of residence of a person.

Absolute title The title refers to the level of ownership of the land or property. An absolute title is the highest form of ownership and means that no other person is better entitled to that land.

ACE Association of Consulting Engineers (governing body of engineers).

Acknowledgement of service When a claim has been issued, the party against whom the claim is brought will need to file an acknowledgement of service where he is unable to file a defence of the claim within the required time frame.

Act of God An event that occurs outside of human intervention and is due to natural causes, such as a storm or earthquake.

Adjudication A quasi-judicial form of dispute resolution that is used mainly in the construction industry, usually as an interim form of dispute resolution. It allows for disputes to be resolved whilst works continue and for a final determination of the dispute to be decided at court at a later date should the parties so wish.

Affidavit A statement of evidence "sworn" by the party making it.

Agent A party or person employed to act upon another party or person's behalf.

Agricultural tenancy The cumulative sections of agricultural land comprised in a tenancy contract, provided the land is not let to the tenant whilst he is employed by the landlord. The tenant must have 12 months notice to quit.

Alternative dispute resolution (ADR) These are non-adversarial forms of dispute resolution where the parties try to negotiate a settlement either between themselves or through an independent third party acting as a mediator.

Annuity An annual payment of a sum of money.

Capacity A party must be "capable" of entering into a contract. Therefore minors and those with a mental disorder are not considered capable of entering into legal contracts.

Cause of action A series of facts or events that give rise to a right of action against another party(s).

Caveat Warning.

Caution (Restriction) A party with an interest in land may register a caution (restriction) against the land so that it is made aware of any dealings in that land.

Certified copy A true copy of the document certified by a solicitor.

Charge A form of security, this can either be over property (such as a mortgage) or over documents.

Chattel Any property other than freehold land.

CIOB Charted Institute of Building.

Compulsory purchase order An order authorizing an authority to forcibly acquire land.

Conservation Area An area designated as being of special architectural or historical interest.

Consideration In contract law some consideration must be paid in order for the agreement to be valid. Consideration is some benefit, it is usually expressed in financial terms, "consideration" must be paid by one party (A) to another party (B) where B has undertaken some act, loss or detriment in order to complete an agreement.

Contributory negligence Where the actions of a party that has suffered some damage or injury due to the actions or inactions of another party contributed to the extent of his damages by his own actions or inactions. Any award is usually reduced to reflect the extent of the contributory negligence.

Copyright The exclusive right in those works. These can be literal, artistic, musical etc. An author of the works usually retains the copyright in the works but may give the employer (for example under an architect's appointment) a licence to use those drawings for the property.

Covenant An agreement to carry out an obligation. This is normally by deed.

Curtailage The vicinity of.

Debtor A party to whom one owes money or is required to perform an obligation.

Default judgement A judgement filed in favour of a claimant where the defendant has failed to file a defence or an acknowledgement of service

Deposition A statement of oath given and signed by a witness in legal proceedings.

Development plans Plans prepared by the local authority that set out the basis for development decisions for the locality.

Disclaimer A refusal to accept responsibility.

Duress Unlawful pressure upon a party to carry out an act. A contract signed under duress is not a valid contract.

Equity This literally means "that which is fair". For example, the courts may decide that the actions of a party were wrong in equity or may give an award on an equitable basis.

Forbearance Failure to exercise legal rights by a party to an agreement.

Gazumping Where the seller pulls out of a transaction

before contracts are exchanged because he has a higher offer from another buyer. An immoral but otherwise legal act.

Hire-purchase agreement Where a party hires the goods for a term and then, provided he has complied with the hire agreement, has the option to buy the goods at the end of the term. Hire-purchase agreements are governed by the Consumer Credit Act 1974.

House of Commons The "lower" house of the Houses of Parliament which is occupied by elected members.

House of Lords The "upper" house of the Houses of Parliament which is occupied by Lords and Ladies. These appointments are hereditary or by Government.

ICE Institute of Civil Engineers.

Indemnify Where a party has made obligation to make good a loss or expense suffered by another party, that party is said to have indemnified the other party.

Injunction This is an "order" issued by a court (at its discretion) obligating a party to carry out an action or to prevent or cease an action being carried out.

JCT Joint Contracts Tribunal (prepare standard forms of construction contracts).

Lien The right for one party to hold the property of another party until the performance of an obligation is complete. For example a lawyer has a lien over his clients file and documents until his fees are paid.

Limited company A company whose liability is limited to the value of its shares or guarantee.

Limited title guarantee See *Absolute Title*. Limited title guarantee is where the seller of a property does not warrant that it has absolute title (for example there may be a squatter that has rights in the property).

Liquidated A fixed amount; the opposite term is unliquidated.

Quarter Days Christmas Day (25 December), Lady Day (25 March), Midsummer Day (24 June), Michaelmas Day (29 September). (Different dates apply in Scotland.) These days mark the beginning of each quarter of the year. Traditionally these have been the days when accounts are settled and typically with commercial properties, these are rent days.

Repudiation Where a party acts in such a way that he no longer believes that he is bound by terms of the contract.

Rescission Termination of the contract either by the parties or the court. If a contract is rescinded the parties no longer have any obligations under that contract.

RICS Royal Institute of Chartered Surveyors.

RIBA Royal Institute of British Architects.

Retention of Title A clause in a contract where the seller attempts to retain ownership in the goods despite the goods having been delivered to the buyer.

Time of the essence Where the completion of a task pursuant to a contract must be completed within a certain timeframe, then this timeframe is a condition of the contract.

Ultra vires An act which exceeds the lawful power given to that party or body. This results in the act being void.

Vexatious litigant A person who habitually brings action to court where he had no reasonable chances of success. Such a person may be restrained from bringing further actions.

Warranty A declaration or assurance.

Without Prejudice Correspondence marked "Without Prejudice" means that the correspondence cannot be adduced in evidence by the other party in the event of court proceedings.

Useful Contacts

ADJUDICATION

www.adjudication.co.uk

BUILDING (magazine)
www.building.co.uk
www.tonybingham.co.uk

ARCHAEOLOGICAL FINDS

THE COUNCIL FOR BRITISH
ARCHAEOLOGY
www.britarch.ac.uk
Tel: 01904 671417

ENGLISH HERITAGE
www.english-heritage.org.uk
Tel: 0870 333 1181

INSTITUTE OF FIELD
ARCHAEOLOGISTS
Tel: 0161 275 2304

BUYING AND SELLING

COUNCIL OF MORTGAGE
LENDERS
www.cml.org.uk
Tel: 020 7437 0075

LAND REGISTRY
www.landreg.gov.uk

CONSTRUCTION

ASSOCIATION OF CONSULTING
ENGINEERS (ACE)
www.acenet.co.uk
Tel: 020 7222 6557

THE CHARTERED INSTITUTE
OF BUILDING
www.ciob.org.uk
Tel: 01344 630700

CONSTRUCTION INDUSTRY
COUNCIL (CIC)
www.cic.org.uk
Tel: 020 7637 8692

HEALTH AND SAFETY
EXECUTIVE
www.hse.gov.uk
Tel: 08701 545500

INSTITUTION OF CIVIL
ENGINEERS (ICE)
www.ice.org.uk
020 7222 7722 (main
switchboard)

THE JOINT CONTRACTS
TRIBUNAL LTD
www.jctltd.co.uk
Fax: 020 7637 8670

CONSTRUCTION
WARRANTY PROVIDERS

BRITISH PROPERTY
FEDERATION
www.bpf.org.uk
Tel: 020 7828 0111

NATIONAL HOUSE-BUILDING
COUNCIL (NHBC)
www.nhbc.co.uk
Tel: 01494 735363 (customer
services for non-claim
enquiries)

ZURICH MUNICIPAL
www.zurich.co.uk/municipal/Z
MHome/Welcome.htm
Tel: 01252 522000

DISPUTE RESOLUTION

THE CENTRE FOR EFFECTIVE
DISPUTE RESOLUTION
www.cedr.co.uk/
Tel: 020 7536 6000

COURT SERVICE
www.courtservice.gov.uk/
Tel: 020 7210 2266 (customer
service unit)

LORD CHANCELLOR'S
DEPARTMENT
www.lcd.gov.uk
Tel: 020 7210 8500

ENVIRONMENT

ENVIRONMENT AGENCY
www.environment-
agency.gov.uk

WASTE MANAGEMENT
LICENSING REGULATIONS
www.hmso.gov.uk/si/si1994/U
ksi_19941056_en_1.htm

GENERAL

COMPANIES HOUSE
www.companies-house.gov.uk
Tel: 0870 33 33 636

GUY ELYAHOU
buildinglaw@tiscali.co.uk

INSTRUCTING SOLICITORS

LAW SOCIETY OF ENGLAND AND WALES
www.lawsociety.org.uk
Tel: 020 7242 1222 (main switchboard)

NATIONAL ASSOCIATION OF CITIZENS ADVICE BUREAUX
www.adviceguide.org.uk

PARTY WALLS

THE PYRAMUS & THISBE CLUB
www.partywalls.org.uk
Tel: 028 4063 2082 (administration office)

ROYAL INSTITUTE OF BRITISH ARCHITECTS (RIBA)
www.riba.org/
Tel: 020 7580 5533 (main switchboard)/
0906 302 0400 (public information line)
RIBA BOOKSHOP
www.ribabookshops.com
Tel: 020 7251 0791 (to order by phone)

THE ROYAL INSTITUTION OF CHARTERED SURVEYORS (RICS)
www.rics.org/
Tel: 0870 333 1600 (for general enquiries)

PARTY WALLS ACT
www.hmso.gov.uk/acts/acts19 96/1996040.htm
www.partywalls.com/

PLANNING

HIGHWAYS AGENCY
www.highways.gov.uk
Tel: 08457 50 40 30

HOUSE BUILDERS FEDERATION
www.new-homes.co.uk/
Tel: 020 7608 5100

ORDNANCE SURVEY
www.ordsvy.gov.uk
Tel: 08456 05 05 05 (helpline for general public enquiries)

PLANNING INSPECTORATE
www.planning-inspectorate.gov.uk
Tel: 0117 372 6372

THE TOWN AND COUNTRY PLANNING (GENERAL PERMITTED DEVELOPMENT) ORDER 1995
www.hmso.gov.uk/si/si1995/UKsi_19950418_en_1.htm

TAX AND VAT

HM CUSTOMS AND EXCISE
www.hmce.gov.uk
Tel: 0845 010 9000 (national advice service)

INLAND REVENUE
www.inlandrevenue.gov.uk
Tel: 020 7667 4001 (general helpline)

THE INSTITUTE OF CHARTERED ACCOUNTANTS
www.icaew.co.uk
Tel: 020 7920 8100 (main switchboard)

Index

abatement notices, statutory
    nuisance 55–6, 137
abortive fees 8–9
acceptance, offers 77–8
adjudication, resolving
    disputes 120, 126–8
Agricultural Holdings
    certificate 34, 35–6
appeals
    enforcement of planning
        controls 43–5
    planning consent 39–41
arbitration, resolving disputes 123
archaeological finds,
    planning consent 51
architects
    abortive fees 9
    disputes 120–1
    final account 106
    instructions to contractor 89–90,
        101–3
    interim certificates 103
    JCT Home Builders contract 162
    making a planning application 35
    plans 59, 61
    practical completion certificates 95
    professional bodies 59
    professional indemnity
        insurance 62, 122
    role of 58
    site inspections 98–9
    site meetings 98
    varying contracts 101–3
    see also professionals
Areas of Outstanding Natural
    Beauty 46, 151, 153, 155
Association of Consulting Engineers
    (ACE) 59, 68, 164
assured short-hold tenancy 134–5,
    137
auctions 77

bankruptcy 14, 17, 122, 129
banks
    collateral warranties 71–6
    financial advisers, 13
    see also mortgage lenders
barristers 9
bills of quantity 90
boundaries, party walls 156, 159
breach of condition notice, planning

consent 43
breach of contract
    alternative remedies 121–2
    Building Regulations 52
    collateral warranties 71–6
    completion 24
    damages 93
    misrepresentation 140
    negligent statements 142–3
    remedies for 24, 84–6
    resolving disputes 120–30
    specific performance 86–7, 121
    time limits 121, 122
    viability of claim 122
bridging loans 14
British Property Federation (BPF), 76
Building Act (1984) 28–9
building contracts
    clauses specific to 89–97
    see also contracts; Joint Contracts
        Tribunal (JCT)
Building Regulations 26, 51–2, 131
building societies
    financial advisers 13
    see also mortgage lenders
building works
    building contracts 69–71
    designs 59–62
    insurance 62
    planning 58–65
    programming 104–5
    site administration 98–101
Buildmark scheme 62, 76, 95–6
buying land 10–25
    completion 12, 22
    exchange of contracts 12, 19–21
    finances 12–14
    post-completion 12, 22
    post exchange/pre-completion
        12, 20–2
    pre-exchange of contracts 11–12,
        14–19

Capital Gains Tax 14, 132
capital repayments, mortgages 14
Centre for Dispute Resolution
    (CEDR) 126
certainty, offers 78
chained transactions 19, 24
change of use, planning consent
    29–31

Chartered Institute of Building 127
children, safety 101
Citizens Advice Bureau 8
civil law 6
cladding, planning consent 149
coal mining search 17
collateral warranties 71–6, 114,
    115, 131
commonhold land 11, 12
commons registration search 17
Companies House 129, 163
company search 17
compensation
    breach of contract 121
    consumer rights 110
    enforcement of planning
        controls 45
    negligence 122
    see also damages
completion
    contracts 12, 21–2
    breach of contract 24
    completion statement 21
    conditional contracts 19
completion, practical (PC) 95–6
completion notices, planning
    consent 38
compulsory purchase orders (CPOs)
    17
conciliation, resolving disputes 123,
    126
conditional contracts 18–19
Conservation Areas, planning
    consent 28, 46–8, 146, 151, 153,
    155
Conservation (Natural Habitats)
    Regulations (1994), 146
consideration, contracts 78
Construction (Design and
    Management) Regulations
    (1994) 99
Construction Industry Council 127
Construction Products Regulations
    (1991) 69
construction works
    building contracts 69–71
    designs 59–62
    insurance 62
    planning 58–65
    programming 104–5
    site administration 98–101

consultants *see* professionals
consumer contracts, unfair terms 82–3
Consumer Protection Act (1987) 111
consumer rights 107–12
contaminated land 53, 54–5, 56–7
contingency sums 103
contractors
  all-risks insurance 62, 70, 122
  architect's instructions 89–90
  building contracts 69–71
  clauses specific to building contracts 89–97
  collateral warranties 71–6, 114, 115
  and consumer rights 107–8
  contract law 77–88
  design-and-build contractors 59–60, 62, 69, 71
  final account 106
  insolvency 62–3, 65, 122, 129
  interim certificates 103–6
  JCT contracts 162
  letters of intent 79
  nuisance 117
  offers 77–8
  partnership agreements 74–5
  performance bonds 67, 71
  practical completion (PC) 95–6
  quotes 59, 61–2
  resolving disputes 120–30
  site meetings 98
  staged payments 70
  tenders 64–7, 77
  traditional method 59, 61–2
contracts
  claims for loss and expense 92–4
  clauses specific to building contracts, 89–97
  conditional contracts 18–19
  contract law 77–88
  damages for delayed completion 94–5
  defects liability period 95, 96
  delays 90–2
  design-and-build contracts 121
  exchange of 12, 19–21
  extensions of time 90–2, 95
  managing 101–3
  misrepresentation 140–2
  no contract 92
  performance 83–4
  practical completion (PC) 95–6
  practical considerations 87

professional appointments 68–9
Scottish law 165
signing 87, 163
tenancy agreements 135
termination of 96–7
terms 79–81, 124
third party rights 84–6
unfair terms 81–3
variations 89–90, 99, 101–3
see also breach of contract; Joint Contracts Tribunal (JCT)
Contracts (Rights of Third Parties) Act (1999) 76, 84
contributory negligence 122
conveyancers 11
conveyancing 10–25
copyright licences, designs 68, 76, 164
CORGI-registered gas engineers 137
costs *see* finances
Council for British Archaeology 51
Council of Mortgage Lenders (CML) 13
County Court 6, 123, 125, 128–9
Court of Appeal 6
court orders, resolving disputes 128
courts, resolving disputes 123–5, 128–30
covenants, restrictive 16, 34
criminal law 6
Crown Courts 6
Crown Prosecution Service (CPS) 6
Customs and Excise 63

damages
  breach of contract 24, 84–6, 93
  defective services 110
  disputes 121
  late completion of works 89
  liquidated damages 91, 92, 94–5
  misrepresentation 141–2
  negligence 113
  negligent statements 142–3
  nuisance 119
dangerous products, liability 111
deeds, purchase 21
Defective Premises Act (1972) 135
defective services 110
defects, consumer rights 108–10
defects liability period 95, 96
delays
  buying land 22–4
  contracts and 90–2
deleterious materials 68–9

deliveries, signing for goods and materials 109–10
demolition, planning consent 28–9
Department of the Environment 55
deposits 12, 14, 19–20
design-and-build contractors
  contracts 69, 71
  designs 59–60
  disadvantages 60
  disputes 121
  professional indemnity insurance 62
designers *see* architects
designs
  copyright licences 68, 76, 164
  planning construction 59–62
disputes
  party walls 160–1
  resolving 120–30
drainage pipes 56
driveways, planning consent 33, 153, 154
duress, contracts 78–9
duty of care, negligence 113–14, 122

easements 16
enforcement
  environmental law 56–7
  planning controls 42–5
  resolving disputes 128
engineers
  JCT contracts 162
  plans 59
  professional bodies 59
  professional indemnity insurance, 62
  role of 58
  see also professionals
English Heritage 51
Environment Agency 53, 55, 56
environmental law 53–7
  contaminated land 53, 54–5
  enforcement 56–7
  general responsibility 53–4
  regulatory bodies 53
  statutory nuisance 53, 55–6
environmental searches 18
environmentally-friendly houses 55
estate agents, deposits 19–20
European Court 6
European Union 82, 111
eviction, tenants 137, 138–9
exchange of contracts 12, 19–21
experts, resolving disputes 125, 129

INDEX

express terms, contracts 79, 80
extensions
  listed buildings 49
  and party walls 156–61
  planning consent 26, 35, 146–55

failed transactions, remedies 24
faulty goods, consumer rights 108–9
fees
  buying land 13–14
  professionals 13, 69
  solicitors 8–9
fences, planning consent 33
final account 106
finances
  buying land 12–14
  completion 21–2
  contractors' quotes 61–2
  cost management 103
  costs of litigation 129
  fees 8–9, 13–14
  final account 106
  financial advisers 13
  interim certificates 103–6
  planning consent appeals costs 41
  staged payments 70
  see also compensation; damages;
    fines
fines
  breach of Building Regulations 52
  water pollution 56
fire safety 137
fixtures and fittings, sale of property
  131–2
flats
  commonhold 12
  leasehold 11
force majeure 83, 91
foundations, party walls 156,
  159–60
freehold land 11–12

gas appliances, safety 137
General Permitted Development
  Orders (GPDO) 21–3, 35–6, 146

health and safety, site administration
  99–101
Health and Safety at Work Act
  (1974) 99
Health and Safety Executive (HSE)
  99–100
High Court 6, 41, 123, 125, 128, 129
hire purchase agreements 82
holiday accommodation, tenants 138
home extensions see extensions

House of Commons 6
House of Lords 6
Housing Act (1985) 137
Housing Act (1988) 134

implied terms, contracts 79, 80–1
injunctions
  enforcement of planning
    controls 43
  for nuisance 119
injuries, liability to visitors and
  trespassers 100–1
insolvency, contractors 62–3, 65,
  122, 129
Institute of Civil Engineers (ICE) 69
Institute of Field Archaeologists 51
insurance
  buying property 20
  construction works 59
  contractor's all-risks insurance
    62, 70, 122
  professional indemnity insurance
    62, 68, 122
  public liability insurance, 62, 70,
    122
interest payments, mortgages 14
interim certificates 103–6

Joint Contracts Tribunal (JCT)
  contracts 81, 95, 162–4
  Agreement for Minor Building
    Works (1998) 70
  Building Contract for
    Homeowners and Occupiers
    (1999) 69, 70
  claims for loss and expense 93
  Homeowners/Occupiers Contract
    with Consultant's
    Appointments (2001) 162
  Intermediate Form of Building
    Contract (1998) 70
  liquidated damages provision 91
  Standard Form of Building
    Contract with Contractor's
    Design (1998) 69, 71
  Standard Form With/Without
    Approximate Quantities 71
  variations 89–90
land, buying 10–25
land ownership
  commonhold land 11, 12
  freehold land 11–12
  leasehold land 11–12
  Scottish law 165
Land Registry 14, 15–16, 22, 156
landlord and tenant 134–9

Lands Tribunal 39
Latin terms 166
Law Society of England and Wales
  8, 9, 19
lawyers see barristers; solicitors
leasehold land 11–12
letters of intent 79
liability
  contracts 80, 81, 83, 85
  dangerous products 111
  site visitors and trespassers 100–1
licence of occupation 134
liquidated damages 91, 92, 94–5
listed buildings
  enforcement of planning
    controls 42
  extensions 49
  planning consent 28, 46, 48–50,
    146, 149
  VAT exemption 63
loans, bridging 14
  see also mortgages
local authority
  development plans 35, 36, 38, 51
  environmental law 53, 56
  planning consent 26–52
  searches 16–17, 22–4
  and statutory nuisance 55–6
losses
  breach of contract 84–6
  claims for 92–4
  liquidated damages 91, 92, 94–5
  mitigating 121–2
  negligence 113–15

magistrates 6
manufacturers, consumer rights 109
mechanical engineers, role of 58
mediation, resolving disputes 123,
  126
meetings, site 98
Misrepresentation Act (1967) 140–2
misrepresentations 140–4
money see finances
mortgage lenders
  collateral warranties 71–6
  and contaminated land 54–5
  deeds 22
  landlord and tenant
    responsibilities 138
  lending criteria 13
  requirements for construction
    works 58–9, 131
  solicitors 14
  surveys 18
  warranties 62–3

mortgages
  redemption 21–2, 132
  terms and conditions 19
  types of 14

National House Building Council
  (NHBC) warranties 13, 17, 114,
  115
  Buildmark scheme 51, 62–3, 76,
  95–6
  mortgage lender requirements 59,
  62
  premiums 63
  selling houses 95–6, 131
  Solo scheme 62–3
National Parks, planning consent 46,
  151, 153, 155
negligence 113–16
  duty of care 113–14
  landlord and tenant
    responsibilities 135
  pure economic loss 114–15
  resolving disputes 121, 122
negligent statements 142–4
negotiation, resolving disputes 122,
  125–6
neighbours
  nuisance 117–19
  party walls 156–61
noise, nuisance 117, 119
notice period, tenants 135
nuisance 117–19
  character of area 119
  damage caused 119
  landlord and tenant responsibilities
  135–7
  remedies, 119
  rule of Rylands and Fletcher 118

Occupiers Liability Act (1957) 100
Occupiers Liability Act (1984) 101
offers, contracts 77–8
oil tanks, planning consent 153
oral contracts 77, 121
outline planning consent 16, 19, 26,
  35, 36, 61
ownership of goods 110
partnership agreements 74–5
Party Wall Etc. Act (1996) 156
party walls 156–61, 164
payments see finances
performance, contracts 83–4
performance bonds, contractors 67,
  71
planning consent 26–52
  appeals 39–41

applying for 34–8
  archaeological finds 51
  change of use 29–31
  completion notices 38
  conditional contracts 18
  Conservation Areas 28, 46–8,
  146, 151, 153, 155
  demolition 28–9
  enforcement of planning controls
  42–5
  environmental issues 55
  exemptions 31–4
  extensions 26, 35, 146–55
  listed buildings 28, 46, 48–50,
  146, 149
  outline planning consent 16, 19,
  26, 35, 36, 61
  renewals 38
  retrospective planning consent 42
  sale of property 131
  searches 16, 17
  Section 106 agreements 36, 38–9
  time limits 36–8
  tree preservation orders (TPOs)
  17, 48
Planning Contravention Notice
  (PCN) 42–3
Planning Inspectorate 40
Planning (Listed Buildings and
  Conservation Areas) Act (1990)
  46
planning officers 35, 42, 55
planning supervisors, role of 58
pollution
  contaminated land 53, 54–5,
  56–7
  water pollution 56
porches, planning consent 32, 151
possession, landlord and tenant
  responsibilities 137–8
post-completion processes 12, 22
post-exchange processes 12, 21–2
power of attorney 20, 21
practical completion (PC) 95–6
pre-exchange of contracts 11–12,
  14–20
Premier Warranty 13, 62
professionals
  appointing 68–9
  breach of contract 121
  fees 69
  JCT contracts 162–4
  liability limits 69
  mortgage lender requirements
  58–9
  negligent statements 143

professional indemnity insurance
  62, 68, 122
  role of 58
  tenders 66–7
  VAT 63
  see also architects; quantity
    surveyors; structural engineers;
    surveyors
programming works 104–5
project managers 61
public liability insurance 62, 70, 122
purchase deed 21
pure economic loss, negligence
  114–15

quantity surveyors
  final account 106
  interim certificates 103
  pricing works 61
  professional bodies 59
  role of 58
  see also professionals
quotes
  contractors 59, 61–2
  solicitor's fees 8

rainwater drainage 56
registered land 15–16
rejecting goods 109–10
remediation notices, contaminated
  land 54, 56–7
remedies
  failed transactions 24
  for nuisance 119
rent arrears 138
repairs, landlord and tenant
  responsibilities 135
resident landlords 134–5, 138
restrictive covenants 16, 34
retention
  defects liability period 96
  practical completion (PC) 95
retrospective planning consent 42
rights of way 100
Roman law 6, 165
roofs
  planning consent 147, 149, 151
  skylights 154
Royal Institute of British Architects
  (RIBA) 59, 68, 103, 106, 164
Royal Institution of Chartered
  Surveyors (RICS) 59, 68
rule of Rylands and Fletcher 118,
  119

safety
 landlord and tenant
  responsibilities 135–7
 liability for dangerous products
  111
 site administration 99–101
Sale of Goods Act (1979) 107–8,
 109, 121, 141
Sale of Goods and Supply of
 Services Acts 80–1
sale of property 131–3
satellite antennae, planning consent
 32, 149, 152, 154, 155
Scottish law 6, 165
searches 16–18
 bankruptcy 14, 17
 coal mining 17
 commons registration 17
 company 17
 delays 22–4
 easements 16
 environmental 18, 54
 fees 14
 local authority 16–17, 22–4
 planning history 16
 post-exchange 21
 pre-exchange of contract 14
 restrictive covenants 16
 water authority 17
Section 106 agreements, planning
 consent 36, 38–9
self-build houses
 collateral warranties 76
 professional appointments 68
 warranties 62–3
Sellers Property Information Form
 (SPIF) 17, 131
semi-detached houses, party walls
 156–61
services, defective 110
services engineers, role of 58
sewers 17, 53, 56
signing contracts 87, 163
signing for goods and materials 109
signs, warning 101
site administration 98–101
 health and safety 99–101
 liability to visitors and trespassers
  100–1
 site inspections 98–9
 site meetings 98
skips 55
skylights, planning consent 154
Small Claims "Court" 123, 128,
 129–30
SMR 51

solicitors
 buying land 11–12, 14–25
 complaints 9
 delays 22–4
 fees 8–9
 finding a solicitor 8
 instructing 6–8
 Latin terms 166
 mortgage work 14
 sale of property 132
Solo scheme 62
specific performance, breach of
 contract 86–7, 121
staged payments 70
Stamp Duty 14, 21, 132
statutory nuisance 53, 55–6, 117,
 135–7
stop notices, enforcement of
 planning controls 43, 45
strikes, and contract terms 91
structural engineers
 JCT contracts 162
 plans 59
 professional indemnity insurance
  62
 role of 58
 see also professionals
Supply of Goods and Services Act
 (1982) 108, 109, 121, 141
surveyors
 abortive fees 9
 misrepresentation 141–2, 143
 party wall disputes 161
 see also quantity surveyors
surveys 18
swimming pools 32, 65, 152, 154

taxation
 Capital Gains Tax 14, 132
 Stamp Duty 14, 21, 132
 VAT (Value Added Tax) 63–4,
  103, 133
Technology and Construction
 Court 120
tenancy in common 15
tenant, landlord and 134–9
tenants, joint 15
tenders 59, 61–2, 64–7, 77
terminology, Latin 166
terraced houses, party walls 156–61
third party rights, contracts 84–6
time extensions, contracts 90–2, 95
time limits
 breach of contract, 86–7, 121,
  122
 claims for loss and expense 93

offers 78
 planning consent 36–8
 planning consent appeals 39–40
tort 113, 122, 142–3
Town and Country Planning Act
 (1990) 26, 39
Town and Country Planning
 (General Permitted Development
 Orders) 21–3, 35–6, 146
Trading Standards Departments 109
trees
 in Conservation Areas 47–8
 tree preservation orders (TPOs)
  17, 48
trespassers, on building sites 100, 101

undue influence, contracts 78–9
Unfair Contract Terms Act (UCTA,
 1977) 81–2, 85
Unfair Terms in Consumer Contracts
 Regulations (1999) 81, 82–3

variations, contracts 89–90, 99,
 101–3
VAT (Value Added Tax) 63–4, 103,
 133
visitors, to building sites 100–1

walls
 planning consent 33
 party walls 156–61, 164
warning signs 101
warranties 62–3
 collateral 71–6, 114, 115, 131
 mortgage lender requirements 13,
  62
 sale of property 63, 131
 see also National House Building
 Council (NHBC)
waste management
 environmentally-friendly houses
  55
 waste management licences 53, 55
water companies
 water authority search 17
 water pollution 53, 56
weather, and contract terms 91, 92
witholding notices 106
working hours 163

zero-rated projects, VAT (Value
 Added Tax) 63
Zurich insurance 13, 17, 59, 62–3,
 115, 131